Kindred Spirit, Kindred Care

Kindred Spirit, Kindred Care

Making Health Decisions on Behalf of Our Animal Companions

Shannon Fujimoto Nakaya, DVM

New World Library
Novato, California

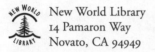 New World Library
14 Pamaron Way
Novato, CA 94949

Interior design by Tona Pearce Myers

Library of Congress Cataloging-in-Publication Data
Nakaya, Shannon Fujimoto.
  Kindred spirit, kindred care : making health decisions on behalf of our animal companions / Shannon Fujimoto Nakaya.
      p.   cm.
Includes bibliographical references and index.
ISBN 1-57731-507-3 (pbk. : alk. paper)
  1. Pets. 2. Pets—Health. I. Title.
SF413.N35 2005
636.088'7—dc22   2005000880

First printing, June 2005
ISBN 1-57731-507-3
ISBN-13 978-157731-507-X

♻ Printed in Canada on 100% postconsumer waste recycled paper

g A proud member of the Green Press Initiative

Distributed to the trade by Publishers Group West

10 9 8 7 6 5 4 3 2 1

For all the animals who enhance our lives

Contents

Introduction

Caring for animals was not just a career choice, it was a calling. Besides healing my animal patients, I have long aspired to do something that would more broadly benefit animals and the humans who care about them. One day, as I reflected on how we make health care decisions on behalf of animals, I realized that the best decisions consider factors besides the patient's medical needs. In the course of twenty years in various aspects of the veterinary profession, I have come across many unique situations and solutions. My purpose for writing this book is to guide people through the process of making the best choices for their animal companions.

Most people love their pets and want them to live long, happy, and healthy lives. As reality has it, however, even the best cared for and deeply loved pets are subject to illness, disease, and eventually death. It is when such events threaten that I hope I can really be of assistance to my patients and their humans. As a veterinarian, I help people make and carry out decisions about their pets based on their own values, resources, and spiritual beliefs.

For those of you who can't believe how much you love your dog or cat — or your bird or horse or iguana or hamster or whatever other animal you happened to connect with and that happened to connect with you — this process will help make the most difficult decisions a little bit easier. Even though it will still be hard on your feeling-self, your thinking-self will know that you are doing the best you can for your loved one.

If you are lucky, you will have to make very few difficult decisions on behalf of your animal companion because he or she will be healthy, live a long life, and then pass away peacefully in his or her sleep. Indeed, an entire chapter is devoted to aging gracefully and the ways that we can increase the odds of this happening for our animal friends. It is also about paying attention to our pet companions as they proceed through their lives. Animals can teach humans many lessons about aging gracefully. Most have fewer hang-ups about the process, or worries about the future, than we do. They enjoy what each day has to offer. If we can respect and learn from that attitude, the quality of all of our lives might improve.

Nevertheless, most of us will at some point be challenged to make decisions of some sort about our pet's health care. These decisions have become much more complex than they were ten or even five years ago because of the increasing variety of options in veterinary health care today. Where there used to be a local veterinarian who took care of everything, there are now numerous specialists for different animals and different types of illnesses. Technology has expanded to include ultrasound, computer tomography (CT or "CAT scan"), magnetic resonance imaging (MRI), nuclear medicine, radiation therapy, chemotherapy, carts and wheelchairs, artificial limbs and joints, dialysis, transplants, pacemakers, hydrotherapy, acupuncture, herbal treatments, and dozens upon dozens of other ways of diagnosing problems and prolonging life. However, rather than survey the ever-expanding multitude of care options, this book will guide you in the best way to make choices no matter what the options are.

Moreover, like humans, animals are living longer, challenging us to redefine "old." When I first started working as a veterinarian, my boss's fourteen-year-old Labrador retriever suddenly collapsed one day with a very painful abdomen. An ultrasound revealed a fluid-filled liver mass, and with much disquiet, a surgeon was called in to explore the dog's abdomen. An abscessed liver lobe was removed and the patient recovered and lived for three more years. The challenge that day was whether to risk surgery, which might not have been successful, or to accept that this illness was the end of fourteen good years of life. No one wants a pet's life to end as a failed medical procedure. But if we succumb to preconceptions about age or refrain from offering patients the best care options because they are "old," it may shortchange them and ourselves the gift of life. Age should be a consideration, but it is not a diagnosis or a disease.

Some of you may choose not to pursue certain medical procedures, whether for philosophical, financial, or other reasons. If you were my client, however, I would present you with options, the likely outcomes, and the possible complications. Why shouldn't the person who lives with, cares for, and most understands and loves an animal be fully informed and participate in deciding its fate? Another chapter in this book is devoted to choosing a veterinarian whose views about pets and health care parallel your own. Most veterinarians want to heal animals, but their approaches, styles, and standards of excellence can vary tremendously. It is easier for you, your pet, and your veterinarian if you share similar goals and philosophies in regard to life and health care. Your veterinarian can guide you, carry out diagnostics, and prescribe treatments, but part of your responsibility as your pet's caregiver is to make the decisions that will affect the quantity and quality of that individual pet's life.

This book is not going to tell you what to do. Instead, it reflects on different views about human-animal relationships, life and death, Western and non-Western medicines, and pet care and commitment. The choices that work for you and your animal companion may differ from the choices that work for me and my animal companion. The choices that work for my socially interactive and accommodating pet may differ from the choices that work for my independent and opinionated pet, even if they happen to have the same medical condition. Neither choice is inferior or superior to the other; they are just different. Every animal's individual interests deserve to be accommodated, and many variables affect our decisions: the animal's ailment, prognosis, personality, and temperament; our relationship with that pet; our lifestyle, priorities, financial resources, and previous experiences; our philosophical and/or spiritual beliefs; and our ability to provide hands-on supportive care. My goal is to help you realize and think through the options available to you and your animal companion and to help you make well-reasoned decisions.

Most of the examples I use in this book involve pet dogs, cats, and birds because these are the species that make up most of my patient population. However, while the details might vary for other species, the processes and principles I present can be extrapolated and applied. I should also clarify that my focus is on those human-animal relationships where a bond or some emotional attachment already exists. In more institutional human-animal interactions — for example, those based on production or research — the fate of animals is decided based upon different goals and priorities. While I am sympathetic to the plight of animals in these situations, it is the subject matter of a different book. Perhaps by better understanding the animals with whom we share our daily lives, we will better appreciate and seek to help the other animals with whom we share the planet.

The terms we use when describing humans, animals, and their relationship to each other often have subtle and sometimes not-so-subtle connotations and implications. However, this book is not a commentary on animal politics. I do not desire to offend those in favor of granting animals legal rights, nor do I desire to alienate the average "pet owner." My goal is focused on the more practical matter of helping animals as they currently exist in our lives, and I have tried to use neutral, nonpolitical phrasing. When referring to humans in these relationships, I use the terms "human" and "caregiver." When referring to animals, I personally prefer the phrases "nonhuman family member" and "animal companion," though I do use the term "pet" as well — since, all politics aside, that is how most people refer to their companion animals. I also follow the convention common in veterinary settings where humans who come into the office are referred to as "clients" and animals are referred to as "patients."

Kindred Spirit, Kindred Care is the result of my own involuntary pondering during countless walks on the beach and in the forest with my dog. It is my journey into ethics, healing, and spirituality. It is a culmination of my experiences with the many clients who have shared their lives with me and entrusted their animal soul mates to my care. It is a collection of lessons from my animal patients and companions about enjoying life, aging gracefully, and being honest. I hope that our experiences may lead the way for others.

Kindred Spirit, Kindred Care

CHAPTER ONE

Honoring the Human-Animal Bond

Perhaps writing about the human-animal bond in a book titled *Kindred Spirit, Kindred Care* is akin to preaching to the converted. Yet I have met many people who are embarrassed and/or feel compelled to justify and defend their attachment and commitment to an animal companion. Animals have been our partners, protectors, teachers, companions, and soul mates. Search-and-rescue dogs work tirelessly to find human survivors in the wake of disasters. Animals ranging from wild horses to docile bunnies have taught abused children and hardened convicts about nurturing and trust. Dogs, cats, horses, bunnies, birds — even canaries that weigh less than an ounce — have offered company, affection, entertainment, song, and cheer to many humans, including myself, demanding little in return.

Animals are for the most part nonjudgmental, honest, and loyal companions. Pets offer comfort to humans without hesitation, even when other humans shy away or alienate them. More than one client has confided to me that she or he could not have given up an addiction were it not for the pet who sat with them through the darkest hours of recovery. Why is it that society makes us feel compelled to do things for other humans even if we feel they are undeserving, and yet puts us in a position where we need to rationalize, justify, and defend our commitment to the animals who share our lives every day? These are companions who trust us; what does it say about us if we do not respond to them in their time of need?

Most people reading this book already want to do the right thing. But what is right will vary for different people and their different animal companions. Deciding what is right lies partly in the personality, temperament, and interests of the individual animal. Since our animal companions don't usually express themselves through spoken words and language (with the exception of some birds), we must learn to understand their body language, facial expressions, and behavior. Nonverbal communication is so natural that we tend to forget that we communicate nonverbally all the time.

Infant children cannot speak, but most people recognize when they are happy, sad, frustrated, tired, or in need of attention. We often know someone's mood even before he or she says anything, especially if the person is someone with whom we are familiar.

Of course, misinterpretation is possible with nonverbal communication. Suppose your roommate returns home in a rotten mood. With words, you just ask what is up. But if you had to depend on nonverbal communication, you might have to observe for a while to see if the bad mood improves, persists, worsens, or conjoins with other cues that something is amiss. You might have to troubleshoot by offering various aids — food, a blanket, a walk, a game, a hug — and assessing the response. This process of observing and troubleshooting is basically the same whether your roommate is human or animal, and the more familiar you are with your companion, the less likely you are to misinterpret what he or she is communicating.

In some ways, this is even easier with animals because they rarely lie. For a variety of reasons, humans will tell white lies or otherwise hide their true feelings. They might be embarrassed by the truth, or they might be trying to spare your feelings, or they might be telling you what they think you want to hear in order to avoid conflict. So even with language, we sometimes must rely on nonverbal communication to diagnose what is really going on with another person. As the saying goes, actions speak louder than words, and much to their credit, it is not in the nature of our animal companions to act independently of their feelings.

In academic circles, Dr. Jane Goodall was criticized for decades because of her observations of personality, temperament, intelligence, learning, social structure, allegiances, deception, aggression, nurturing, play, humor, and love in chimpanzees. Among many of the academic elite, it was preferable to criticize and dismiss Goodall's work rather than face her findings and conclusions. Critics claimed that Goodall anthropomorphized her subjects; as evidence, they cited the fact that she assigned the chimpanzees names while doing fieldwork. Of course, Goodall's critics also realized that humans historically justified their mistreatment of animals and animal environments by claiming that animals do not possess intelligence, emotion, or awareness, and Goodall's work undermined that claim. Goodall's findings not only linked humans and primates in evolutionary terms but also threatened the supposed human supremacy over all animals and ecosystems.

Since then, other researchers and authors have contributed to the ever-expanding volume of records documenting animal intelligence, creativity, emotion, and other characteristics traditionally ascribed to humans alone. Whether they are citing examples of chimpanzees hiding bananas when more dominant members of their group are present, of the mourning rituals of elephants, of a leopard soliciting help to save her offspring, of parrots putting sentences together, or of orcas grieving a miscarriage, the reports prove what most pet caretakers already know: animals can formulate opinions and act on them. Pets let us know when they are happy or unhappy, comfortable or uncomfortable, bored, in pain, frightened, anxious, or enraged. They let us know when they have a need and, often enough, the nature of that need.

Some animals are more emphatic about their opinions than others, and some humans are better at reading and interpreting nonverbal communications than others. Nevertheless, when humans simply pay attention to animals, animals prove to be undeniably sentient creatures. Even within a flock of parakeets, each one possesses its own levels of confidence, curiosity, vanity, bravery, perseverance, patience, passion, and seriousness. Being familiar with your animal companion Star means understanding that Star is one of a kind and irreplaceable. Cloning might replicate Star's DNA, but not Star. Pet caregivers know that Dr. Goodall's observations are correct.

Acknowledging that animals possess intelligence, awareness, and emotion is not to say that there are no differences between humans and animals. No one expects a dog to design the next space station, a cat to direct brain surgery, or a parrot to run for governor. Humans and animals are physically different, leading to significantly different aptitudes. The neocortex of the human brain is generally more developed than the neocortex of other species. On the other hand, canines generally have a better sense of smell than humans, which is why humans employ dogs to sniff out drugs, explosives, and missing persons. Felines have night vision, retractable claws, incredible athletic prowess, and speed. Most birds have a range of vision that spans almost 360 degrees and a brain that can process these images as they fly. Homing pigeons can navigate many thousands of miles; dolphins can echolocate; camels can store enough water to cross a desert; and vultures can digest substances that kill other species. Human "superiority" is a fabrication of egocentric minds.

Some have argued that human superiority is real due to the fact that we alone have invented ways to exceed the capacity of our physical bodies: we have designed airplanes, automobiles, electric lights, telephones, washing machines, computers, and central heating. This is true, and I admit that I like my mind, my opposable thumbs, and the conveniences of modern life. But we should still acknowledge and respect that all life-forms have desirable attributes, and that intelligence is not the end all. Intellect does not equate to goodness, kindness, generosity, or caring. Along with their intellect, humans are the most destructive creature the planet has ever known. A little humility on the part of the human species will not bring about our demise. Rather, it might lead us to become better stewards of the planet.

In fact, animals have much to teach us about ourselves as individuals and as a species. For one thing, animals teach us to look beyond the surface. My patients don't care what I look like or what I'm wearing; they don't care about my age, gender, race, religion, or sexual preference. They are mostly concerned with how I am going to treat them, and in turn I try to communicate kindness, familiarity, and a sincere desire to help and not harm them. In addition, animals have a natural comfort with their bodies in all of its various shapes, sizes, textures, and smells. Even amputees or patients who have undergone radical surgery are generally not stigmatized by their asymmetry. In turn, people accept, and often even come to adore, underbites, bulging eyes, crooked legs, asymmetric ears, sagging skin, and wrinkled faces.

Animals teach us to think about our actions. Many years ago, an extraordinary veterinary nurse, Hilary Doliber, taught me that when you treat patients with kindness and respect, earn their trust, and ask nicely, most patients cooperate. I have applied Doliber's approach for years, and it works. I never require that patients be separated from their caretakers (that's like kidnapping); I rarely feel the need for muzzles or restraining devices; and I almost never wrestle animals into submission (that's like assaulting a sick person). Veterinary medicine is a profession that requires ongoing thinking and creativity for each individual patient. I continually try to engineer ways of making procedures and treatments more tolerable for patients who don't feel right and might not fully comprehend the motives for our bizarre conduct and requests.

My favorite, however, is that animals teach us about living in the moment, letting go, and enjoying life. Pets diagnosed with cancer don't obsess over their mortality or what is to become of them. For their entire lives, animals carry on from moment to moment and day to day based on what each moment offers. Animals do not harbor regret, and resentments tend to be short-lived. Some humans insist that animals can only live in the moment because of their simple minds, but even if that were true, it wouldn't diminish the lesson. When our human lives become too complicated and burdensome, being able to put our troubles aside, even if only for a moment's reprieve, becomes pretty attractive. My canine companion regularly reminds me about the real joys in life — regular meals, walkabouts, cushy beds, and frequent doses of affection. Through recognizing and accommodating his joys, I maintain a more balanced perspective about the things that are really important in my own life.

There is much more that can be said about how animals enhance our lives. One of the best books ever written about human-animal relationships is Susan Chernak McElroy's *Animals as Teachers and Healers*. I unreservedly recommend this collection of stories and reflections from regular people, who are exceptional only in their appreciation and respect for animals and animal companions. McElroy eloquently brings together their stories, along with countless insights and pearls of wisdom. It is truly an honest and beautiful book about people and animals.

Respectful and thoughtful treatment of animals and animal environments should be a gesture of our own human goodness. Human-animal relationships are largely based on nonverbal communication. By developing our awareness of and capacity for nonverbal communication, we broaden our horizons: we increase our potential for relationships, and we increase our ability to make the right decisions on behalf of our animal companions.

CHAPTER TWO

Healthy Living and Graceful Aging

A lot of people don't like to think or talk about getting old — for themselves or their pets. Like it or not, from the time you're born, you start to age. Life is aging. Death will happen. It is how slowly and gracefully you get there that really matters. Healthy living and graceful aging is about maximizing the quantity and quality of our pets' lives. There are no guarantees. We are just trying to stack things as much in our favor as possible. Discussing how we can achieve healthy living and graceful aging has become central to how I manage my patients.

Enjoying What Each Day Has to Offer

Animal companions can teach us so much about enjoying the simple things in life. Imagine yourself and your pet in a few of the following scenarios: going for a walk, chasing a ball, taking a ride, sharing the couch, eating, reading the paper, tromping across the keyboard, coming home, shopping for toys, scratching, petting, preening, napping, playing, sharing, sniffing, staring into each other's eyes with unabashed love. Like humans, each animal is an individual with a unique blueprint of personality, temperament, talents, likes, and dislikes. Part of the joy of having a pet is discovering and nurturing the special features of that individual, creating an environment where that unique being can thrive, and appreciating how lucky you are to have your life enhanced by him or her.

If you have multiple pets, your relationship with each one will be unique. This makes each pet experience all the more precious. It is normal that you may connect more easily or more intensely with one than another. The important part is understanding and respecting each individual.

Being Fair

The flip side to enjoying the things that make your pet special is recognizing his or her particular needs and accommodating them. If your companion is an athletic, high-energy dog, for example, he or she is going to be much more manageable indoors if you take him or her outside to chase a ball for an hour every day. If your cat is shy and timid, she or he won't want to be dressed up and displayed in cat shows. You cannot expect a macaw or a cockatoo to be quiet and still all the time — they are by nature loud, emotional, demonstrative creatures, and it is not their fault that your apartment doesn't absorb sound as well as a rain forest.

If you adopt a pet when you are in between jobs and home all the time, accepting a position that has you gone for long hours and traveling a lot can mean a difficult transition for any pet. Admittedly, it is difficult to predict what life will deal us, but like most humans, animals prefer some degree of stability in their lives. Part of responsible guardianship is being there for your pet and being fair to your pet.

Education and Good Manners

We are all subject to various societal laws that define and enforce a minimum code of behavior; we might also abide by certain principles and ethics suggested by our religion, culture, or family. These rules allow humans to share home, community, country, and planet. If you take pet guardianship seriously, you might be committing fifteen or more years to a dog, twenty or more years to a cat, thirty years to a cockatiel, or seventy years to a parrot. You need to teach your pet the rules. The goal of pet education is to shape behavior so that your long-term relationship is a joy and not a burden. A proper education will also allow you and your animal companion to be safe and spend more time doing fun things together.

All my dog friends, for example, learn how to walk nicely on a leash. It is unpleasant and unsafe when an overexcited dog tries to chase an ambulance or dart in front of traffic to get to a squirrel on the other side of the road. All of my flighted parakeet friends can be easily "herded" back to their cage when something is happening that might startle or endanger them. Even cats, reputed to have minds of their own, can be encouraged to accept a few rules, such as not attacking their housemates or redesigning all of the furniture.

Once you define your "house rules," you must figure out a way to communicate them effectively to your pet. Sometimes it happens naturally. Your pet does something undesirable, you glare at your pet, he or she gives you a remorseful look, and it never happens again. At other times, when you and your pet are having a communication breakdown, trainers and behaviorists can be valuable resources. Even though I am a veterinarian, I have many times called my dog trainer for insights about my dog's behavior and for advice on what to do about it. I have similarly consulted with bird behaviorists and other behavior specialists for insights into other species. Some pets will really challenge us about a chosen rule. At times, we must pick our battles and do our best.

One thing I have learned is that there are as many ways of training an animal as there are of educating a child. There are training styles that incorporate discipline or negative reinforcement and those that use only positive reinforcement; there's the dominance approach and the bribery approach; and there are food motivators, clickers, gentle leaders, pinch collars, citronella collars, scat mats, spray bottles, noisemakers, whistles, and many other training devices to choose from. Some animals, like some children, figure out the rules no matter how they are presented. Some animals respond only to one approach and not at all to others. Equally important, if you are uncomfortable with a style, it will not work.

For example, when I was teaching my dog to sit, one trainer taught me to give the command "sit" as I held my dog's collar in one hand and pushed on his rump with the other, then to praise and reward him once he was in the correct position. Another trainer believed this method was too imposing. Her method was to use a piece of food to motivate the dog to look up; eventually the dog would end up in the sit position because it is more comfortable to sit than to stand when you're a dog with your nose way up in the air. At this point, the trainer would praise the dog and offer the reward. The latter method is certainly gentler and works great for some dogs, but not for others. When offered food, some dogs will sit and then stand a half second later, or they never sit, or they jump up and leap for the treat, or they sit and bark and then think that they are being rewarded for staring at food and barking rather than sitting. Then again, the hold the collar and push on the rump method that worked for my dog will make some dogs startle and turn or spin as soon as they feel your hand on their body, while some animals drop their entire bodies to the ground, and some drop and roll over. Different strokes for different folks, as they say, and for different pets.

There are many trainers out there to choose from. When selecting a trainer, request an interview and ask questions. Visit the school if there is one and observe its methods and results. To me, a good trainer is one who does the following:

- Knows several ways to teach a rule.
- Understands your animal's temperament.
- Understands what is motivating undesirable behaviors.
- Appreciates your preferences.
- Chooses the style that best fits you and your animal companion.
- Continually reevaluates and makes customized adjustments throughout the training process.

I advocate teaching all pets at least a few minimal "house rules," but some pets thrive on advanced education. Discovering and developing your pet's talents can enhance the bond between you. When you train together, you and your animal companion learn to function as a team.

Diet and Exercise

When it comes to your pet's health, diet and exercise are the two easiest things to control, and they can have a significant impact. There are many overweight pets in America, and excess weight increases health problems, speeds up aging, and shortens lives. Most diabetic cats are obese. Most dogs that require back surgery are obese. Obese Amazon parrots are about as likely to have high cholesterol and to suffer strokes and heart attacks in their middle ages as comparably weighted humans. If your pet has an underlying predisposition toward heart or respiratory disease, obesity will certainly exacerbate the condition. Obesity will cause arthritis to develop sooner and progress more rapidly. Obesity complicates recovery from anesthesia and surgery.

Of course, lean patients can also develop these problems. As I've said, there are no guarantees: we can just try to improve our odds. Dachshunds and corgis and other dogs with short legs and long backs, for example, are structurally predisposed to back problems. (Don't think I'm picking on dwarf breeds. I love these dogs. I live with one.) You can decrease the odds of having a problem by keeping them lean and fit, keeping their nails trimmed so they have traction, and building ramps in place of stairs wherever possible. Even with all of these preventives, your pet could still develop a back problem, but hopefully one that will respond to rest and medical management rather than one that will force you to decide whether or not to pursue an emergency CT or MRI and surgery on a Sunday afternoon or render your canine companion permanently paralyzed and incontinent. Healthy living not only helps to minimize the incidence and severity of problems, it also improves the likelihood of recovery, and shortens the duration of healing.

There is no health risk to being lean. Ideal body weight is dependent on individual bone structure and conformation. A scale can be helpful, but you don't need one to determine whether or not your pet is the ideal body weight. You can assess the situation based on look and feel. For dogs and cats, when you look at your standing pet from above, he or she should have a slight hourglass figure between shoulders and hips. Bulges in the middle are unnecessary weight that slows down your naturally agile pet.

Bird body conformation can also be assessed by feel, though it is a little trickier than with mammals. Birds have a keel bone down the middle of their chest. There are muscles on each side of the keel bone. You should be able to feel your bird's keel bone at the same level as the muscles, or just slightly protruding. Your veterinarian can help you figure out your bird's body conformation. If your bird is overweight, it might be helpful to purchase a digital gram scale so that you can monitor changes from day to day.

Obesity in pets saddens me because it is so easily remedied by balancing caloric intake and energy output. The daily quantity of food recommended on the back of a pet food bag is just that, a recommendation. In my experience, many adult pets require less than the "recommended" volume of kibble. The recommendations do not factor in the treats that your pet gets in between meals. Dog biscuits can be a deceptively dense calorie source. A four-inch-long bone-shaped cookie can weigh as much as a half cup of kibble and contain an equal number of calories. Rawhide is not calorie-free. Neither are pig ears or snouts or any other livestock body part that is smoked and marketed as a snack. All of the snacks that your pet is getting need to be included in calculating his or her total caloric intake.

Given the opportunity, most pets will consume more calories than they require. After all, one of the goals of pet food companies is to make the food irresistible. And people love to indulge their pets. When clients say to me, "But Comet seems so hungry," what they really mean is that Comet seems so happy when they offer food, and it makes them happy when Comet is happy. But if Comet is getting heavier every year, you are not really doing him justice in the long run. Always keep in mind that you do not have to compromise your own or Comet's happiness in order to maintain an optimum body weight.

If your pet is overweight, here are some of the suggestions I usually give, not necessarily in the order that you should try them. My basic premise is to adjust the volume of calories that your animal companion consumes each day without changing his or her routine. A few cautions: First, if your pet has been placed on a special diet for any reason, check with your veterinarian before making any additions or changes to what you are offering. Second, if your pet is consuming fewer calories than seems reasonable and still has a weight problem, check with your veterinarian. Third, never subject a pet to a starvation diet. If your pet needs to lose weight, it should do so gradually. An obese patient that does not eat for several days can develop a potentially life-threatening condition called hepatic lipidosis. And finally, water has no calories and should not be restricted to control weight.

1. Get a measuring cup. Most people don't know exactly how much their pet is consuming each day. Measuring cups are cheap. Just keep one in the food bin. Measure how much your pet is being offered. Maybe this amount is actually more than you thought.

2. Get lower calorie food. There is no shame
   in doing so. It means that your pet is more
   fuel efficient, like a subcompact car —
   lucky you! Less active formulas have the
   same balance of nutrients with fewer calories.
   Also, get smaller treats. Your pet is less
   likely to notice a decrease in the size of his
   or her treats than a decrease in the number
   of treats per day. Birds can be dieted in the
   same way, and oftentimes simply eliminating
   the high fat foods will do it. Seeds and nuts
   are not essential food items to parrots.
   They are fun to eat and tasty, and this is
   why many birds prefer them over other
   food items that are more nutritious but less
   fattening.

3. Decrease the volume of kibble per serving.
   Whether you offer your dog one cup of
   kibble or two-thirds of a cup of kibble, it's
   going to be gone in thirty seconds anyway.
   Do not change the number of feedings:
   doing so will be noticed.

4. Add fillers. If your pet really objects to the
   decrease in kibble volume and gives you
   that look, replace the volume with carrots,
   pumpkin, or green beans. These can be
   fresh or canned, raw or steamed, or whole,
   chopped, or shredded. Be warned that

fillers increase poop volume. If your pet picks the kibble out from between the fillers, well, that's his or her choice; it suggests that your pet is not really starving. Raw carrots crunch much like dog cookies, and they are acceptable low-calorie replacements for many pets.

5. Add water to kibble. This will expand the volume of the kibble — filling up more space in your pet's tummy.

6. Exercise. You can eat more if you burn more calories. Exercise will also build muscle mass and increase cardiovascular strength. It might also become a means for you and your animal companion to spend more quality time together. When it is a frigid winter day in New England, my dog is so happy to be out running through the snow that I bundle my tropic-born body into layers of clothing just to share in his joy. In the summer, we swim. In the spring and the fall, we go for walks in the woods. Most neighborhoods have loosely organized doggie playgroups that meet early in the morning before people go to work. Doggie day care programs have evolved in some places. Some people prefer more organized activities like agility, herding, search and

rescue, or field trials. It doesn't matter whether your dog actually competes in these activities or not, as long you are having fun together. Some cats will chase a flashlight or motorized mouse. Birds can also be exercised. Depending on the size of your bird and your lifestyle, some birds can remain flighted. Flying is amazing and burns lots of calories. For other birds, being fully flighted comes with significant risks and is not an option. Wing flapping, walking, running, and dancing exercises can be great forms of aerobic activity and entertainment for both you and your feathered friend. Be creative.

7. Make regular time to tell your animal companion how special he or she is. Food should not be a substitute for love.

Being Observant

Being familiar with your pet's physique and idiosyncrasies is an important part of a preventive health care plan. Consider your pet named Ginger. What do Ginger's eyes look like? Are they clear? Is there any redness? Do they tear? What does it look and smell like under those floppy ears? What color are her gums? How do her upper and lower teeth meet? Are her teeth securely rooted, clean, and white? How far around her muzzle does her tongue reach? Does Ginger drool? What is her body conformation? How does she carry her head? How far back can it reach? How far to each side? Is her chest broad or narrow? How does her belly hang? Does her back arch or sag? How does Ginger move? Notice the coordination of all four limbs and the motions of each step. Watch her curl herself into a ball and notice how much each joint flexes. Watch her stretch and notice how far each limb can extend. Feel her coat. Notice her skin. Are there areas with more and less fur (or feathers)? Are there areas with more pigment and less pigment? Noticing what is normal for your pet makes you more astute in recognizing when things are not normal.

Equally important, remember that for Ginger, actions don't speak louder than words; actions are her words. Pay attention to her behavior and habits. Does Ginger prefer cool weather or warm weather? Is she a morning creature, an evening creature, or an anytime creature? Is she food motivated or food indifferent? Is she an athlete or a couch potato? What is the normal color and consistency of her bowel movements and urine? What is her normal energy level? When it comes to discomfort, is she stoic or sensitive? Does she react indifferently or dramatically to change? Is she sensitive or indifferent to your mood swings? Knowing what is normal for your animal companion allows you to determine earlier on when something is amiss, which allows in turn for earlier diagnosis and treatment, less progression of the problem, and general better living for your pet.

Grooming

By grooming, I don't mean the poofy doos of the show dog world. If those aesthetics make you and your pet feel special, then great, but I am more concerned with the grooming that contributes to the health and longevity of your pet — mainly teeth and toenails.

It is a myth that if pets consume only dry food, they will not develop dental disease. More and more pets are now living long enough that they develop severe dental problems, and not just in terms of bad breath and cavities. Dental tartar starts off as that slimy substance called plaque that you feel on the surface of your teeth when you wake up in the morning. Crunching on hard food (if your pet doesn't just swallow his or her food whole) will remove some of it, but a certain amount of that plaque will still cling to the teeth, especially along the gum line on the cheek-side surfaces of the upper teeth. Over time, that plaque will mineralize and harden into tartar. Millions of bacteria get trapped in the space between the tartar and the gums.

Several outcomes are possible. Cavities can develop. If the cavity penetrates into the central root canal of the tooth and bacteria enter the canal, a root abscess can occur. Some patients demonstrate discomfort at this point. Others demonstrate an amazing tolerance for dental conditions — they don't miss a meal even as teeth abscess, rot, and fall out. As a result, dental disease may not be perceived as a problem. However, complications can develop, usually when the patient is older and has other health issues. Sometimes tooth abscesses extend beyond the tooth and form draining tracts to the nasal cavity or the side of the face. Of greater concern, the bacteria trapped between the tartar and the gums can seed infections to other parts of the body. Heart valves and kidneys are known targets.

Numerous commercial products are marketed to help with your pet's dental hygiene, though success varies for each individual pet. Some dogs will spend hours gnawing on bones or chewing toys, while others can't be bothered with these objects; certainly, having them lie around the house does not prevent dental disease. As a veterinarian, my greatest concern is the individuals who chew so aggressively that they fracture their teeth or swallow large pieces that necessitate surgical retrieval. Even the chews labeled as 100 percent digestible may not pass through the intestinal tract without causing significant discomfort and irritation if ingested whole or in large pieces. I have extracted teeth that were fractured on hard beef bones, induced vomiting in dogs who have ingested so much rawhide in one sitting as to be visibly distended, and performed emergency surgery to retrieve pieces of hard rubber toys that were causing an intestinal obstruction. Because of these experiences, I strongly advise supervision when introducing something new to your pet. If it starts to look like a disaster waiting to happen, throw it away and try something else.

By increasing the size and hardness of the kibble, some diets are designed to clean teeth as your pet chews. However, if your dog or cat does not chew his or her food (that is, you do not hear any crunching during mealtimes), then these diets will not help your pet's teeth at all. Even if your pet chews once or twice, it may not be enough to get the full benefit intended by the diet.

Pet toothpaste, toothbrushes, dental wipes, and mouthwashes are also available and can be helpful for some individuals. Be warned that if your pet bites down on the toothbrush, a wicked tug-of-war game can ensue. Pet toothpaste was helpful in introducing the concept of teeth cleaning to my dog, but when he became so enthusiastic about the toothpaste that it was a battle to get past his eager licking tongue, we had to abandon it for unflavored wipes.

To me, there is no substitute for just wiping the slimy plaque off the surface of your pet's teeth with a hand towel. It might take a little effort to get your pet used to the idea and the routine, but it is worth trying. More pets than you might imagine will tolerate this process, which takes just a few seconds. Because plaque most commonly accumulates on the cheek-side surfaces of the upper teeth, your pet does not need to open his or her mouth in order for you to keep these critical surfaces clean. In fact, it is better if your pet keeps its jaws closed during cleanings so that you cannot get bitten, even accidentally. The technique starts with desensitizing your pet to having fingers in his or her face and lips, and then gradually progressing toward teeth wiping. Some pets will progress through the stages in a few weeks; others will take longer. Be patient. If your pet demonstrates anxiety or fear, stop immediately. Clean teeth contribute to healthy living, but not if the process causes excessive stress to you or your pet.

Toenail trimming is another grooming activity that often gets overlooked in caring for pets. When toenails get too long, they interfere with ambulation. Dogs and cats are supposed to stand and walk on their toe pads. When toenails get too long, the angle of the toes and feet is shifted, and nails rather than pads touch the floor. Or sometimes the nails will curve and grow into the pad, resulting in painful sores. This latter problem is most common in older cats that no longer scratch and wear their claws down independently. The altered conformation, decreased traction, and/or sore toes can lead to slipping and falling, sprains and bruises, and more serious orthopedic injuries.

Like teeth cleaning, toenail trimming should never be a traumatic event for you or your pet. Start by getting your pet used to having his or her feet touched. Gradually progress to picking them up one at a time, feeling in between toes, and touching each toenail.

Don't forget to pet the rest of the animal at the same time; there is no point in arousing suspicions. Whether you, a groomer, or a veterinarian does the actual toenail trimming, this exercise will still make it easier and less stressful for your pet.

Humans approach life and the need to care for themselves in a myriad of ways, and we can extend that creativity to our animal companions. Through careful observation and flexible solutions, I try to make healthy living and graceful aging minimally imposing and maximally rewarding for my animal companions. There are no guarantees, but we do our best and hope that we will be blessed with many healthy years together.

CHAPTER THREE

Choosing a Veterinarian

I read an ethics article recently that broached the question of how extensively older patients should be diagnosed and treated. A veterinarian observed that his own fifteen-year-old cat had a slightly decreased appetite and a tiny bit of weight loss — 10 percent by the scale. When blood tests, X-rays, and ultrasound were all normal, the veterinarian decided to anesthetize his cat and biopsy its intestinal tract. Thus he learned that his cat had lymphoma, a type of cancer. A year later, when his cat was still alive and thriving with the help of chemotherapy, he started to present the case to other veterinarians. His point was that in pursuing an aggressive workup in a not-so-sick patient, he had diagnosed his cat's condition earlier and was able to put her cancer into remission. The article went on to describe his surprise at the negative responses he'd received from other veterinarians, who'd felt that a fifteen-year-old cat was clearly past its prime and such extravagant diagnostics and heroic treatments were unnecessary. This story clearly exemplifies one of the heavy topics of disagreement about pets and indicates the broad range of value systems that exists among veterinarians, as well as among pet owners. Whatever your personal values, it is helpful to find a veterinarian who shares them, or at least can willingly accommodate them.

Personal Values and Medicine

Traditionally, doctors of Western medicine have assumed a paternalistic approach to diagnosing and treating patients. This attitude derives from the idea that Western medicine is based on science and that doctors understand that science and medicine in a way that laypersons cannot. For the sake of physician efficiency, clients and patients are kept less informed of the medical process and are expected to comply and get better. This approach is more tolerable when there is a rapidly diagnosed and cured problem. When the outcome is less certain, however, a paternalistic approach can lead clients and patients to feel that they have been deceived and manipulated by an incompetent physician.

Moreover, as science and medicine have evolved, there are more diagnostic and therapeutic options to choose from. Choices for a cat with renal disease, for example, might include blood tests, urine tests, X-rays, ultrasound, biopsy, transplant, dialysis, diuresis, special feeding, hospitalization, feeding tubes, medicines, and transfusions. Depending on the cat, the client, their relationship, and the client's resources, not to mention the client's spiritual and ethical beliefs, the best choices for each individual will be different. If decisions are based only on science, with the goal being longevity, our pets will be reduced to nothing more than furry test tubes and research animals.

My own approach to veterinary practice aims to educate clients and present them with all the options. It seems to me that this style is more flexible in that it respects and accommodates a broader range of values. Of course, even this approach does not work for everyone. If clients do not want to understand and think about the physiologic processes occurring in their pets — or if they've already decided what's wrong and what treatment is necessary before they even schedule the appointment! — they will not appreciate this approach.

Even when your veterinarian presents you with options, those options are still subject to that veterinarian's values and experiences. Take myself, for example: I don't believe in vaccinating six-week-old puppies with modified live virus vaccines; I don't crop ears; I don't take unnecessary anesthetic risks; and I will not surgically impregnate an animal. I don't endorse treating unchecked arthritic dogs with aspirin. While I respect the goal of keeping pets comfortable, I have witnessed too many geriatric patients bleeding uncontrollably as a complication from aspirin therapy — a risk I am not willing to take. My approach to aging joints starts with a physical examination to evaluate the patient's overall health, conformation, activity level, range of motion, and degree of discomfort. If indicated, blood work and/or radiographs might be recommended. I encourage weight management, physical therapy, hydrotherapy, nutritional supplements, acupuncture, regular exercise, heat, and massage — all with the intention of minimizing drug therapy. If an individual does require ongoing drug therapy, the patient is scheduled for regular checkups to monitor for efficacy and side effects. As much as I try to provide clients with options, there are some options and practices that I am not comfortable with. If those happen to be options that a client prefers, then I usually suggest the individual find a veterinarian who can support his or her values.

Levels of Training and Types of Veterinary Practices

One trend that I have observed in recent years, at least in cities and more densely populated regions, is an increase in the number of veterinary specialists and specialty practices. In order to become a licensed veterinarian, one must fulfill several requirements: (1) successful completion of a doctor of veterinary medicine degree (DVM) at an accredited veterinary school; (2) achieve passing scores on two national exams; and (3) achieve passing scores on state exams in the state(s) where he or she desires to practice. For better or for worse, internships and/or residencies are not a required part of a veterinarian's training.

Historically, most veterinarians ended their formal training at the level of the general practitioner and rose to the occasion when patients with special needs presented themselves. In recent years, there have been more opportunities for veterinarians to formally advance their training and become recognized as specialists, similar to specialists in human medicine. These veterinarians enter into three- or four-year-long residency programs (or officially sanctioned equivalents) where they concentrate on certain types of cases. They may additionally engage in research, academic writing, and/or teaching. Once their residency is completed, they may take a board exam for that specialty. Once this is passed, they are allowed to practice as a board-certified veterinary specialist.

Boarded specialists used to be congregated primarily at teaching hospitals, but more of them are now offering services in private and corporate veterinary practices. As with any other health care professional, there are things to keep in mind when working with a specialist. First, specialists are still subject to their own biases. Suppose your pet has a lump. A surgeon might recommend surgery; an oncologist might recommend radiation and chemotherapy; and a naturopath might advise herbs, nutrition, and acupuncture. Second, specialists are trained to have expertise in diagnosing and treating specific problems; other knowledge and interests may have gotten archived. Moreover, depending on the practice, specialists do not always communicate well with one another. I once spoke with a surgeon who wanted to perform a fancy reconstructive surgery on a patient, unaware that the patient had a serious clotting problem. Meanwhile, the internal medicine doctor, an expert in clotting disorders, was advising against surgery without ever seeing the injured body part, which clearly required some form of surgical attention. Rather than pooling their expertise and resources, they were each speaking solely from their specialist perspectives and so were giving inadequate advice. Much like a symphony, you can have amazing musicians, but you still need a conductor in order to make music.

Another current trend is a rise in the number of corporate-owned veterinary practices and a decrease in the number of independent, private practices. On the plus side, the largest of these corporate practices and hospitals can usually share resources, have more money to invest in state-of-the-art equipment, and can purchase supplies in bulk quantities at lower costs. They can also more readily offer round-the-clock sophisticated veterinary care. However, it is less likely that one or two familiar veterinarians will be directly involved and accountable for everything that happens to your pet from admit to discharge; it is more likely that a number of people will be involved, and they will be doing their jobs according to established hospital protocol. There can be less flexibility for certain patients and clients. Some patients tolerate standardized care better than others.

Finding a Veterinarian

Given all this information, how do you go about finding the right veterinarian for your animal companion(s)? Start by determining your priorities. Yes, it would be nice to find a veterinarian who is skilled at everything, honest, timely, likeable, accommodating, good with your animal companion, has all the latest equipment, is nearby and available 24/7, charges reasonably, and has an awesome support staff. If you come across this perfect veterinarian, let him or her know how special he or she is.

More likely, you will have to decide what traits are most important to you and work from there. Is it training and experience? I know veterinarians who are immensely talented but who have abrasive personalities, always run behind schedule, or are very financially driven. I know veterinarians who are open-minded to alternatives and integrative medicine and those who are not. As we saw at the beginning of this chapter, there are veterinarians who believe in early detection and those who would assume a more conservative wait-and-see approach. There are veterinarians who believe that life is sacred and should always be prolonged, as well as those who think that diagnosing and treating older animals is a waste of medical resources. There are veterinarians who treat their own animals as members of the family and those who maintain more defined boundaries between animals and humans. There are veterinarians who will make choices for you and simply tell you what to do, and those who will provide information and options and let you decide what would work best for your animal companion.

Once you have determined which traits are most important to you, start looking and asking. In most cases, a general practitioner will become your primary care veterinarian, if not your complete care veterinarian. She or he is someone you should feel comfortable with. I am unaware of a comprehensive list of all licensed and practicing veterinarians. However, most clients find their veterinarians, particularly general practice or primary care veterinarians, via the phone book or by word of mouth. If you are looking for a specialist, then you can start with the organizations that certify them. A list of those websites, including regional listings, has been included in the appendix. Not all specialties have organized board certification, especially those that focus on certain species or on alternative healing styles. Nevertheless, it may be preferable to you to find a veterinarian with at least some interest and familiarity within a certain subgroup of veterinary practice.

Whether it is a generalist or a specialist that you are trying to evaluate, the process is similar. Once you have a list of veterinarians to consider, start learning about them and their practices. Call the practice and ask them to send you any descriptive pamphlets. Check out their website if they have one. Arrange for a visit or a tour, and ask if you might meet the veterinarian. Keep your priorities in mind as you evaluate the practice and the specific doctor. If both seem to your liking, schedule a "new patient" appointment for your pet. This gives you an opportunity to observe the veterinarian in action with your animal companion (and allows you to solicit your animal companion's opinion), and it allows the veterinarian to meet your animal companion as a healthy pet and have something to compare to should a problem arise in the future.

Finding a veterinarian with whom you are comfortable is much like finding anyone else with whom you would like to have a good working relationship. I close this chapter with a secret tip: sharing a short story or something special about your animal companion helps veterinarians get to know him or her more like you do, as a kindred spirit beyond the sum of his or her body parts. Providing the care that preserves these human-animal bonds is one of the greatest rewards of my profession.

CHAPTER FOUR

Assessing the Patient

Whoen a problem arises, things will go much more smoothly for you if you already have a veterinarian you and your animal companion trust. Then, in order for both you and your doctor to make smart decisions, you need information. Good decisions are based on good facts. Patient assessment means gathering the essential facts about your animal companion and his or her symptoms or ailment.

In medical terms, identifying a patient's ailment is called getting a diagnosis. Having a diagnosis helps doctors in several ways. It helps us to understand what is happening in the patient's body to cause the symptoms that you are observing. It helps us to select a treatment plan for the patient that is more likely to work and less likely to do harm. It helps us to predict the outcome — the likelihood of recovery, recurrence, and/or complications — and to recognize when things are going amiss. In short, having a diagnosis assures us that we are treating your pet appropriately.

Getting a diagnosis is a sleuthing process. Consider, for example, that your pet is vomiting. The following sidebar lists ailments I have diagnosed in which vomiting is a symptom. There are other diseases that can also cause vomiting. I just wrote down the seventy-five or so that I personally have observed. Clearly, the seriousness of the problem and the type of treatments required for vomiting patients due to parasites, a foreign body, liver disease, or cancer would be very different.

Ailments That Can Cause Vomiting

Bacterial Gastroenteritis	Drug Reactions
Salmonella	Antibiotics
Clostridium	Antifungal Drugs
Small Intestinal	Cardiac Drugs
Bacterial Overgrowth	Opiates
Biliary Obstruction	NSAIDS
Chlamydophila	Corticosteroids
Diabetes Mellitus	*Ehrlichia*
Diaphragmatic Hernia	Food Intolerance
Dietary Indiscretion	Foreign Body

Fungal/Yeast Infection
  Aspergillus
  Candida
Gastroenteritis
Gastrointestinal Atony
Gastrointestinal Stasis
Hair Ball
Hyperadrenocorticism
Hyperthermia
Hyperthyroidism
Hypoadrenocorticism
Inflammatory Bowel
  Disease
Intussusception
Leptospirosis
Liver Disease
  Chronic Hepatitis
  Hepatic Lipidosis
  Iron Storage Disease
  Hepatic Neoplasia
  Cholangiohepatitis
  Biliary Obstruction
Lyme Disease
Malnutrition
Mycobacteriosis
  (Avian Tuberculosis)
Neoplasia
  Adenocarcinoma
  Leiomyoma
  Leiomyosarcoma
  Lymphoma
  Mast Cell Tumor
Pancreatitis
Parasites

Ascarids
Cestodes
Trichurids
Strongyles
Peritonitis
Protozoal
  Coccidia
  Giardia
  Toxoplasma
  Trichomonas
  Cryptosporidia
Pyloric Stenosis
Pylorospasm
Stress Response
Toxicity
  Lead
  Zinc
  Pyrethrins
  Poisonous Plants
  Chocolate
Ulcers
Uremia
Vaccine Reaction
Vestibular Disease
  Canine Idiopathic
    Vestibular Disease
  Motion Sickness
Viral Infection
  Canine Parvovirus
  Feline Coronavirus
  Pacheco's Disease
  Proventricular
    Dilitation Disease
  Influenza Virus

Sometimes the answers are in the details. Your ability to provide detailed information about an animal companion's normal habits and symptoms can potentially minimize the number of tests necessary to get a diagnosis. For this reason, any information that you disclose to your veterinarian is likely to prompt a dozen more questions as the doctor narrows the list of possible ailments. Text Box 2 is a list of the questions that come to mind when clients report to me that their pet is vomiting.

Questions about Vomiting

1. What is in the vomit?
2. Is it projectile vomiting or more like burping or regurgitation?
3. How frequently is it occurring?
4. How long has it been happening?
5. Has his/her appetite changed?
6. What is his/her normal diet? Is there a recent change in diet?
7. Is there any change in her/his water intake?
8. Is there any diarrhea?
9. Is there a change in energy level?
10. Is there weight loss?
11. Does the pet live indoors, outdoors, or both?
12. Has s/he been to the kennel recently?
13. Do you have any new pets?
14. Have any other pets been affected?

After the interrogation comes a physical examination where both you and your veterinarian's observational skills are put to the test. Your veterinarian's training and experience enable him or her to detect abnormalities in animals, but that ability can be complemented by your familiarity with your pet as a family member, especially if your pet is not a frequent visitor at the veterinarian's office. I learned a long time ago that clients who insist something is amiss with their animal companions are usually correct; even when I can't detect any specific abnormalities about the patient during a physical examination, something will be revealed through a blood test or other diagnostic test. Familiarity with your animal companion will help in the opposite situation as well. I recently examined a cat with a misshapen and somewhat bulbous nose. Upon seeing it, I was very concerned that it was a tumor of some sort; however, the cat's caregiver insisted that it had remained unchanged and not bothersome to the patient for over a decade. The client's knowledge about her pet's unique feature saved us all from having to perform an unnecessary diagnostic procedure.

The information you provide and the physical examination should generate a top ten list of possible diagnoses. Based on this list and the severity of your animal companion's condition, your veterinarian can make recommendations about how to proceed. Numerous diagnostic aids are available to help determine what exactly is ailing your animal companion. Diagnostic aids vary in invasiveness, specificity, reliability, risk, stress on the patient, and cost. Here are some questions to consider when deciding on diagnostic options:

1. What does the test require from your animal companion?

2. How invasive is the procedure? Fecal exams, urinalyses, plain radiographs, ultrasound, and blood pressure checks are noninvasive. Phlebotomy for blood tests and fine needle aspirates are considered minimally invasive. Exploratory surgeries and biopsies are considered invasive.

3. Will it require sedation or anesthesia? Certain types of radiographs require sedation to position the patient correctly. CT scans, MRI, endoscopy, and surgical biopsies require anesthesia.

4. What are the risks?

5. What information is this going to get us? Is it necessary?

6. Will the information change what we do?

7. Are there any other options?

Generally, procedures that are less invasive, less risky, and less stressful on the patient are preferred. At times, however, definitive answers cannot be obtained without an invasive procedure requiring anesthesia or a procedure that will challenge your pet to tolerate some unpleasantness. In these cases, the importance of the information in helping your animal companion needs to be weighed against the risks and costs to him or her. For example, anyone who has undergone a contrast upper gastrointestinal (UGI) or barium study knows the unpleasantness of swallowing gulps of barium followed by hours of waiting in between the numerous X-rays that follow. Under ordinary circumstances, no one would want their beloved pet to have to endure the same protocol; however, if the patient has been vomiting so much during the past month that he or she is losing weight, and other noninvasive tests have not illuminated the problem, then perhaps a UGI will provide information that will save his or her life. The same evaluation should be done when considering any diagnostic procedure.

And while we absolutely want to diagnose what's going on so that we can fix the problem, we must also assess the patient's overall condition so that we don't select a treatment plan that will potentially harm him or her in some other way. For most veterinarians, this overall assessment is mostly worked into the diagnostic process. The patient's medical history, physical examination, blood tests, and other diagnostics provide information about which systems are healthy and which systems are compromised. Suppose your pet is diagnosed with a kidney infection warranting a few days of intravenous fluids and antibiotics. Generally, the goal in these cases is to flush all the toxins and bacteria out of the kidneys, and generous volumes of fluid are administered. Now suppose, in addition to having a kidney infection, your pet's heart is a little feeble. While I don't like finding extra problems in any of my patients, we need to pay attention to these conditions as part of our overall patient assessment. We don't want to discover the problem only after the patient collapses during treatment. Having an overall patient assessment allows us to customize our treatment options and avoid complications. In this patient's case, we might choose to administer fluids more slowly or add medications to support the heart.

Yet another aspect of overall patient assessment is patient tolerance. Now here is a fine line. Most patients, both human and animal, would rather not be poked and prodded, made to swallow gigantic pills or foul-tasting concoctions, or have people hovering about monitoring their every intake and output. A hospital is no one's preferred hangout. Most humans tolerate unpleasant procedures and protocols because they understand the reasoning behind them and want to be well. We can extend this thinking to our animal patients, and in fact kindness, compassion, patience, and competent technical skills can go a long way in negotiating their cooperation and tolerance. Even when you ask nicely, however, patients still exercise different degrees of resistance. Suppose your pet is really difficult to medicate. He or she hides, struggles, tries to bite, gags, and refuses to eat just in case you thought of adding drugs to his or her food. Long-term success sometimes depends on picking your battles. If he or she were my patient or animal companion, I would want to know that the prescribed medication is absolutely necessary and will really make things better, even if additional diagnostics are required to have that higher level of confidence.

Sometimes, diagnostics enter the realm of being academic, meaning that they won't change what can or will be done for the patient in terms of treatment. For example, one of my patients has a very unusual coagulation problem that causes serious spontaneous bleeding. This patient has been tested and retested for all of the recognized and treatable coagulation disorders. Veterinary research institutions have offered further testing to learn more about this patient's unique and unusual condition. Regardless of what is determined, there are currently no new treatment options that will be helpful to the patient. Thus, the testing is academic more than practical.

Diagnostics also enter the realm of the academic when they would only lead to recommending treatments that go beyond what you and your animal companion are willing to pursue. Suppose your animal companion has a tumor in her chest. Maybe it is a slow-growing tumor or maybe not; maybe it is a benign tumor or maybe not; maybe it can be removed surgically or maybe not; maybe chemotherapy will shrink it or maybe not; maybe radiation therapy will shrink it or maybe not. The answers to these questions may become clearer with a biopsy of the tumor, but that would require anesthesia and sticking a needle into the pet's chest cavity. If the tumor did prove to be responsive to surgery, radiation therapy, or chemotherapy, would you pursue any of these options? If you would, then performing the biopsy is an essential diagnostic. If you would not, then performing the diagnostic will not change what you would do for your animal companion, and it would be purely academic.

Academic diagnostics are not necessarily a waste of resources. They can contribute valuable information toward what is known and understood about particular ailments in particular species. While the diagnostic may not help an individual, it might contribute to the field's database of information and extend the boundaries of medical knowledge. It might help another patient down the road. Academic diagnostics can prove beneficial in other ways as well. For instance, in the preceding example, suppose that a biopsy revealed a bacterial colony in the center of the tumor. Prescribing an appropriate antibiotic for the patient might not make the tumor go away, but it might prevent it from filling with pus and rupturing. In addition, by determining the specific type of tumor, you can better predict how the patient's condition will progress and plan accordingly. Sometimes knowing definitively that an animal companion has a terminal ailment makes decision-making easier as his or her condition deteriorates.

Veterinarians can offer professional opinions and recommendations about the best way to diagnose and eventually treat an ailment, but all diagnostic procedures on pets require client authorization. For better or for worse, you bear decision-making responsibility on behalf of your animal companion from the beginning. There is no specific formula for whether or not, or when, to pursue a diagnostic test. It is relative, based on your pet's condition and tolerance and on your need to know.

Getting a diagnosis can be a challenging and sometimes frustrating process. Troubleshooting any system is more complicated when the problem occurs infrequently or intermittently without a consistent prompt or pattern. Although I have diagnosed the specific cause of many sneezes, coughs, limps, runny eyes, itchy feet, smelly ears, dry skin, plucked feathers, bad breath, soft stools, leaking urine, burps, hiccups, farts, tics, and twitches, some cases have remained totally elusive.

One of the greatest underestimations I have ever made was concerning the complexity of the living body. I started veterinary school with the attitude, "It's a finite system. How hard can it be?" As a matter of fact, contained within the body are an infinite number of complicated proteins and biochemical reactions. We understand a lot of these processes, but even more have not been completely figured out. Meanwhile, countless things can go wrong, some of which we understand better than others. Western medicine is applied science, and doctors are limited by the progress of our understanding of how life works, the diagnostic tools available to us, and the treatment protocols that have been worked out and demonstrated to be effective. I don't mean to be discouraging. Medicine and doctors do have value. We just need to acknowledge and understand their boundaries and limitations and keep our expectations in check.

We should also remember that there is value in knowing what an ailment is not—not infectious, not metabolic, not cancerous, not life-threatening. For instance, I recently had a mysterious bump removed from my dog's mouth. I had not seen anything quite like this bump before and neither had any of the veterinarians I showed it to (one of the benefits of being a veterinarian is that you can solicit many opinions). It did not bother my dog (except for all the annoying veterinarians looking at it), nor did it appear to have any of the characteristics of life-threatening bumps; but then again, it can be hard to tell just by inspecting the outer surface of lumps and bumps.

After some deliberation, I opted to have the bump removed, deciding that in the event it proved to be a cancerous bump, early detection would mean better treatment options and greater chances for long-term survival. So the bump was surgically removed and handed over to the pathologists to scrutinize under the microscope. As it happened, they could not determine exactly what it was either. However, they were able to determine that it was completely removed, not cancerous, not life-threatening, and not likely to recur. And that's good enough for me and my dog.

Making health decisions on behalf of our animal companions begins with noticing when things are different with them and working with our veterinarian to fully assess the situation. Patient assessment includes identifying and understanding the ailment as well as the patient's overall condition. We might also consider the patient's tolerance for procedures and protocols, as well as how the information might affect what we do for the patient. Good patient assessments are the foundation for thoroughly understanding care options and making informed decisions.

CHAPTER FIVE

Understanding the Diagnosis and the Options

Once you have a diagnosis and an overall clinical assessment about what ails your animal companion, you can begin to determine therapeutic or treatment options. Before moving too far ahead, however, it is very important that you understand the diagnosis. What is happening in your pet's body? What will happen if we do nothing? Is there a cure? Or is this a problem that we must learn to live with and manage?

If there is anything you do not understand, ask your veterinarian to explain it again or to recommend another source of information. Even if questions arise the next day or the next week, keep asking till everything is clear and makes sense. Sometimes clients come to me frustrated and seeking a second opinion because they don't know what is going on with their pets. In some of these cases, the diagnosis is clearly established in the medical records that they provide me, suggesting that their veterinarian is clinically competent, but somehow the information has not been successfully conveyed to the client.

It takes a lot of time, energy, patience, and practice to communicate effectively with clients from a wide variety of backgrounds, and as in any profession, some veterinarians have better communication skills than others. In addition, a client's emotional involvement and anxiety can decrease his or her ability to receive information no matter how effectively it is presented. However the miscommunication occurs, assigning blame is not productive. Stay focused on the main objective — to make good decisions on behalf of your animal companion — and do whatever you need to do to understand what is happening. Prepare yourself before every discussion, and challenge your veterinarian to explain things in a way that you can comprehend.

Along with the diagnosis, your veterinarian is likely to provide you with suggestions about what can be done to help your animal companion. If you trust your veterinarian and your pet's ailment is clear-cut, uncomplicated, likely curable, and unlikely to develop into a more complicated condition, then you won't need to deliberate very much. It will be easy to decide on the best, most obvious treatment. If, however, the diagnosis is more complicated or the outcome less certain, then before you can make good decisions on behalf of your animal companion, you need to gather information about all the available treatment options.

So as not to overlook any options, I suggest that you consider four categories of treatment: (1) Medical, (2) Surgical, (3) Alternative or Integrative, and (4) Innovative or Experimental. There may be more than one option in any category or none in a category. But if you ask your veterinarian, "Are there medical options given my animal companion's diagnosis? Are there surgical options?..." and so on, you will bring focus to your investigation and are likely to compile a comprehensive list of options.

For each treatment option, you should answer the following questions.

1. What are the likely benefits?
2. What are the potential side effects and complications?
3. Are there prerequisites or restrictions for receiving this treatment?
4. Where is this option offered?
5. When could your pet be accommodated?
6. How many appointments are generally involved?

7. Does this option involve hospitalization?

8. Does this option involve anesthesia?

9. Will this option create special needs at home?

10. What does follow-up involve?

11. What is the financial cost?

Write down all of the answers and information as you talk with your veterinarian; in order to stay organized, I suggest dedicating one page to each option. It is a lot of information to process at one time, especially when newly burdened with the knowledge that your beloved companion is not well. However, as long as your pet is clinically stable and comfortable, then you will not have the added pressure of urgency — another reason to seek an early diagnosis. Admittedly, we don't always have this luxury. Even when we are paying attention to our animal companion's health, emergencies can happen and challenge us to rise to the occasion and do our best. Hopefully, you will have time to gather all the information that you need to make the best decisions on your pet's behalf.

Your primary care veterinarian may not have all of the answers. Some fields, like veterinary oncology or cancer therapy, are changing so continually that it is difficult for the general practitioner to keep abreast of the most advanced protocols. Also, veterinary training is predominantly based on Western medicine. As a result, most veterinarians do not have adequate training in, or knowledge of, herbs, acupuncture, chiropractics, homeopathy, or other "alternative" approaches. For complete answers to all your questions, you may need to contact other sources.

If you are seeking more information or services than your veterinarian can provide, request a referral or a consultation with a specialist. Referrals require your and your pet's physical presence at an appointment. Obtain copies of your pet's medical record, imaging, and test results in advance so that you can get the most out of the allotted appointment time. Without all of the relevant details, it is much more difficult for someone reviewing a case to answer effectively all of your questions or to make specific recommendations. Alternatively, a consultation involves your veterinarian doing the homework and then communicating the information to you. Modern communication allows veterinarians all over the country to share cases and benefit from the knowledge and experience of specialists for particular ailments and therapies. While consultations may involve professional fees, you may get all the information you need without having to transport your pet. Asking for a referral or a consultation does not mean you dislike your veterinarian and don't want him or her to be involved in your pet's care. It means you want to broaden your horizons and be confident that you have left no stone unturned in considering options on your pet's behalf. (As a start, you might investigate the organizations listed in the appendix, or visit my website, www.kindredspiritkindredcare.com, particularly for alternative medicine.)

You may get lucky and find the specialist you are seeking locally, but the current reality is that it may require a day trip to meet with an expert about a particular ailment or species. Often you can learn a lot over the telephone. The staff that answers the phone is accustomed to fielding questions pertaining to their doctor's qualifications and experience. These client liaisons can be a valuable source of information about procedures, protocols, scheduling, and costs. Some specialists offer limited phone consultations directly with clients. Keep in mind, however, that regardless of knowledge and experience, veterinarians cannot diagnose or treat a patient based on a telephone conversation. In order to benefit from the specialized offerings, you will need to schedule an appointment.

Libraries can be a source of general information. However, you may not find the newest editions of books on the shelves. In a field that is changing rapidly, information published ten years ago may be outdated. Veterinary school libraries are a wealth of information, but for lay readers the material and medical language can range from unfamiliar and confusing to overwhelming. If you need a specific answer to a limited question, it may not be worth the effort to find it in this way.

The Internet is a phenomenal source of information, but it must be used with caution. Search engines can instantly gather a wide variety of information on a topic, but they don't evaluate if it's good or bad information. Always consider the source, the context, and if possible, the originator's motive for sharing. For example, one client presented me an abstract (scientific articles are often summarized in this format) that he found on the Internet about a new cancer chemotherapy protocol, and he wondered why I had not recommended it for treating his cat. Only in the last sentence of the abstract was it revealed that the suggested protocol was actually an experiment. The word "experiment" wasn't used in the title or elsewhere in the abstract; hoped-for benefits were emphasized, while there was no mention of the possible side effects or complications. Experimental protocols can be legitimate options, but the uncertainty of the outcome should be clearly understood. (Experimental options are discussed further below.) Misrepresented information offers false promise to hopeful pet caretakers who are unfamiliar with scientific writing styles.

Similarly, online chat rooms and bulletin boards can provide a lot of information, but remember that these usually represent just one person's experience. Recall the long list of ailments that can cause vomiting in chapter 4. Just because an ailment was diagnosed in one patient with similar symptoms, or just because a treatment worked in one patient with the same ailment, does not necessarily mean that it will be so for your animal companion. The information could be useful — don't ignore it — but consider who is presenting the information and then cross-reference it and/or confer with your trusted veterinarian. Remember that each animal is a unique entity.

Considering Alternative Forms of Healing

By far, the most prevalent system of health care in this country is Western medicine. Western medicine is an applied science based on objective knowledge about how a body functions, how diseases alter bodily functions, and how treatments alter diseases. Measurable criteria, statistics, and probability are prominent in scientific analyses. Western medicine did not gain popularity by chance. There is immense value in understanding anatomy, physiology, microbiology, immunology, pathology, pharmacology, and all the other branches of science and medicine that have developed. There is value to the scientific approach, which uses controlled experiments to determine the probability that a test or a treatment is likely, or not, to work.

We must, however, keep our expectations in check. Western medicine has not achieved immortality. (Neither, by the way, have other forms of healing.) As a matter of fact, there are a number of conditions for which Western medicine does not have good solutions — diseases of the immune system, many viral diseases, and many forms of cancer, to name just a few. Unfortunately, in promoting the superiority of their approach to health care, many practitioners of Western medicine have lost sight of the fallibilities of their trade. Clients and patients may not want to hear that their doctor does not know what is going on, or that Western medicine does not have a remedy, but sometimes that is the plain and simple truth. We do injustice to clients and patients by not being honest about the limitations of our trade.

We might also extend our humility so as not to be altogether dismissive of other forms of healing. Lynn Payer's book *Medicine and Culture* compares medicine in the United States to that in several European countries with similar life expectancy. Many medical doctors in Europe include homeopathy in their practice, and most practitioners of homeopathy in Europe have medical degrees. Herbs and homeopathy are more common in German medicine than antibiotics. In France, three-week spa therapy is a legitimate treatment option for certain ailments, such as bronchitis and arthritis. French doctors admit that some of the benefits of spa therapy may be psychosomatic; however, they are not nearly so bothered by this notion as are American and British doctors. The bottom line for the compared populations: similar overall life expectancy. How does it all add up? Western medicine probably has better solutions for some conditions and not as good solutions for others.

It would be great if we could figure out among all the healing systems the world over the best treatment for each problem, but this task is not so simple. Different treatments are based on vastly different understandings of and approaches to health and health care. Sometimes the approaches are so different that it is impossible to build bridges. In traditional Chinese medicine (TCM), for example, it is fundamentally understood and accepted that there is an energy, or *chi,* within each body. Ailments result when that energy's balance and flow are disrupted. Healing is aimed at restoring the balance and flow of *chi,* thereby allowing the body to mend itself. My dog's acupuncturist invested as many years and as much effort learning TCM as I invested in veterinary school. Patients can benefit from acupuncture, but it is nearly impossible to explain *chi* or a TCM diagnosis using the vocabulary of Western medicine. Integrated world medicine, where the best solutions among all healing systems are determined for each ailment, is a tremendously enticing but still-elusive concept.

There are a multitude of alternative approaches to healing: acupuncture, aromatherapy, chiropractic, botanical (herbal), dietary, homeopathy, faith, glandular, magnets, massage, and *reiki,* to name a few. How effective are they? It depends on whom you ask. A majority of doctors of Western medicine have a cultivated bias against other types of healing. Funding to validate the efficacy of alternative approaches is not always forthcoming. We are left with fervent testimonials about alternative treatments from patients claiming successful outcomes, usually backed by the company's marketing department. Some patients have been helped by alternative forms of healing when they could not be helped — or worse, were harmed — by Western medicine. Other patients have been harmed by alternative forms of healing, or they lost an opportunity to do something that would likely have been better. Due to the divide between practitioners of alternative forms of healing and Western medicine, the variable ways of assessing patients, and the different methods for determining and reporting success and failure, alternative treatments are some of the more complicated options to understand and evaluate.

My own approach when considering alternative forms of healing is as follows: If there is a safe, effective, tried, and proven therapy from the canon of Western, science-based medicine, I'd do it. If the outcome from this therapy were likely to be poor, or have significant side effects and/or risk, then I would investigate alternatives. My two big qualifying questions are:

1. Can it harm the patient?

2. Will the patient tolerate it?

One of the guiding principles of my veterinary training was "do no harm" and I try very had to practice by that rule. As for the second question, most alternative forms of healing are geared at restoring balance and supporting the body to heal itself. However, if the patient is too stressed by the process, it will undermine the benefits of the treatment.

Finally, it's worth keeping in mind that some therapeutic benefits in alternative medicine may be derived from placebo and Hawthorne effects. Simply put, the placebo effect refers to patients who improve in response to a placebo or inert medication. Of course, this psychologically based improvement is less likely with pets who are not as cognizant of the medical benefits of pills or injections. The Hawthorne effect explains patients who improve similarly in response to caring and concern. Both the placebo and Hawthorne effects have been statistically demonstrated; a percentage of patients will improve without any particular therapy. What does this mean? To some degree, bodies are designed to heal themselves, and there are health benefits and healing powers in a supportive environment and a positive outlook. Do not overinterpret this statement. Love is not likely to cure cancer. But animals with connections and a reason to live have a greater interest in living, and they tend to live longer. Caring and compassion should be incorporated into all forms of health care.

Understanding Innovative Procedures and Experimental Protocols

One of the ways we advance the boundaries of veterinary medicine is through innovative procedures and experimental protocols. These are, by definition, procedures and protocols that have not been tried and proven. Innovative procedures are usually tailored for an individual patient. Experimental protocols may similarly be individually tailored or may be part of a research project. In the latter, preestablished treatment plans are applied to patient participants who meet very specific criteria. The idea is that by minimizing the variation in patient backgrounds, it is easier to evaluate the actual efficacy of the protocol.

Studies are limited; even when your pet happens to be the correct species with the correct ailment, other conditions may prohibit him or her from inclusion. Even when a pet qualifies, participating in experimental protocols is not for everyone. In double-blind studies, neither you nor your veterinarian is permitted to choose, or even to know, exactly what is being administered to your pet; it may be an existing product, an experimental product, or a placebo. Protocols may require certain tests for monitoring and assessment, and/or they may prohibit other concurrent therapies. While there is usually a theoretical foundation for the experimental protocol and few researchers intend to effect harm through a study, being at the cutting edge of medicine involves many unknowns. If you decide to pursue this type of option, your animal companion will be among the first to experience success or failure. However, no matter what the outcome, you are contributing data that will guide the treatment of future generations of patients.

Before agreeing to an innovative procedure or an experimental protocol, you should know several things: first, you should know about the existing options for your pet's condition and the expected outcomes with those options. Several years ago, a new injectable heartworm preventive was introduced; one injection every six months effectively protected dogs from heartworm disease. At the time, I did not jump to prescribe this preventive because there were already several heartworm preventives on the market that were overwhelmingly safe and effective and generally cost-efficient. And yet, as with many new pharmaceutical products these days, marketing of the treatment was targeted directly at the consumer, resulting in clients requesting this certain product for their pets. For the few patients who were sensitive to the existing preventives or who refused to cooperate during monthly administration of the existing oral products, trying the new product was certainly justified.

Other than that group of patients who might benefit from the new product, however, I did not want my patients included in the generation of test subjects. True, the product had undergone safety and efficacy testing prior to approval for sale by the Food and Drug Administration (FDA); however, all new products undergo another level of "real world" testing after they get FDA approval. Could a product that injected a six-month supply of a drug into a patient be associated with a higher incidence of tumors or cancer ten years down the line? The bottom line is that we don't know, so if there is already a proven product available, why take the risk? Recently, the manufacturer of the product I just described voluntarily ceased production and recalled the product (at the request of the FDA) until further safety issues are resolved.

Second, you should understand the experimental nature of the proposed procedure or treatment. Clinicians want to sound confident and offer cutting-edge, life-saving care to patients. Innovative procedures and experimental protocols can offer hope when the existing options are suboptimal or unlikely to work. As well, clients want to believe that they are providing the best care for their animal companions and want to trust their veterinarians. Under these circumstances, uncertain outcomes can get downplayed or overlooked. Consider the example described earlier about the client who found a new cancer chemotherapy protocol on the Internet. The treatment offered hope for putting the cat's cancer into remission. In fact, it was presented so optimistically that it seemed negligent not to participate. However, at seventeen years of age, the particular patient had compromised kidneys and a heart murmur and was clearly a tad clinically debilitated. Perhaps the chemotherapy would have put the cancer into remission; equally possible was that the chemotherapy would push the patient's otherwise delicately balanced system right over the proverbial edge. It is unfair to clients, patients, and researchers to create false hope, especially when things might not go well.

Which brings me to the third thing you should understand about innovative procedures and experimental protocols. In addition to understanding the hoped-for outcome, you should understand the potential commitment, side effects, and risks. Six years ago, I met a dog with a nerve injury to her foreleg. She could and did use the limb, but since she couldn't completely feel or precisely control how she landed, her foot would get beaten up in the process. Other patients with this type of injury would typically have had the limb amputated; however, this particular patient's people were hesitant to do that and were committed to figuring out a creative solution. Nowadays, several companies manufacture braces, orthotics, and prosthetics for dogs, but at the time, we were designing and making devices on our own. It was not always smooth sailing: we saw each other daily (which is a good way for clients and veterinarians to get to know one another); we were not always successful in preventing blisters or broken bones; and we recontemplated amputation more than once. I confess that even I did not anticipate the complexity of attempting to save her leg. Fortunately, these were, and are, extraordinarily committed clients, and it involved an extremely tolerant patient. A few surgeries, several "sandals," and many custom-made "shoes" and insoles later, she is successfully stomping around on the affected limb. Daily maintenance is still required, and the clients are frequently queried by curious passersby, referring to their dog, "What happened to her foot?"

Nevertheless, with creativity and perseverance, we were able to prove that sometimes limbs injured in this way do not need to be amputated.

Enhancing your understanding about your pet's ailment, the possible treatments, and the probable outcomes helps you to ask the right questions, know better what to expect, and make the best decisions. By empowering you with knowledge and understanding, your veterinarian earns your trust and bolsters your performance as a member of your pet's health care team.

CHAPTER SIX

Financial Commitments

The financial aspect of pet care is a particularly difficult, yet necessary, topic to discuss. On the one hand, there shouldn't be a price tag on the health of our loved ones, human or animal. On the other hand, no health care system, however compassionate, can support limitless free care, and reality has most of us living on a budget. As more advanced diagnostics and treatments become available to pets, the incongruity between pets that have and pets that do not have health care provisions is likely to increase. As harsh as it may seem, health care for many is not a right, but a privilege or a priority.

Sometimes clients express resentment to me about the cost of veterinary care and imply that veterinarians are profit-driven. I can't deny that this may be true for certain individuals — veterinarians are as varied a group as any other — but as a rule veterinary medicine is not the profession by which to get rich. Most veterinarians do not own fancy cars or mansions or stay in five-star hotels. For the first ten to fifteen years of their professional life, many are paying off student loans in excess of $100,000 and trying to eke out a living on what is left. Then, once the loans are repaid, most remain truly very middle class.

Actually, veterinarians offer nearly identical procedures to those performed in human medicine for a fraction of the cost. State-of-the-art equipment is not discounted for veterinarians. Neither are blood tests. In fact, we challenge laboratories to work with smaller volumes of sample on many of our patients, which means that they need to utilize their more advanced and sensitive assays and equipment. At other times, there are variations between species that need to be accommodated. All of which means that it is indeed possible to spend thousands of dollars to get the best care for your animal companion, but most of that money goes toward supporting your pet, not into the pockets of those doing the work. It is neither the money nor the glamour of the profession that motivates most veterinarians. It is the desire to help animals.

Ideally, we should take into consideration and budget for the costs of caring for an animal before we adopt one. Whatever you pay to adopt an animal is just the beginning. Part of being a responsible pet parent involves budgeting for food, bedding, kennels or cages, training, additional security deposit if you are renting, pet care if you intend to go on vacation, and maintenance health care. Additionally, as much as we hope against tragic events, it is a good idea to formulate some financial plan for illnesses or injuries that might suddenly generate significant expenses. Just because an animal is young, purebred, expensive, or well cared for does not guarantee good health. Animals can experience illness at any age. As unjust as it may seem, two-year-olds meticulously cared for and fed organic homemade diets can develop cancer. I know — I've treated them.

Often purebreds have more health problems than mixed breeds. My purebred corgi — supposedly a good specimen of a hearty breed — needed orthopedic surgery when he was seven months old. Then his exocrine pancreas shut down when he was eleven months old, necessitating lifelong supplements. Neither of these conditions was anticipated. Sometimes, we can only rise to the challenges that we are presented with. With a little bit of foresight and planning, there are ways to buffer the financial impact of animal emergencies and unexpected situations. Some people buy pet insurance. Others create their own pet care fund. Some clients have a credit card solely for the purpose of unexpected pet care. Sometimes it is not how much wealth we have, but how we choose to manage and spend it.

There are several things that you should know about pet insurance if and when you select a policy for your pet. First, in most of the currently available plans I have reviewed, you are free to choose whomever you want for a veterinarian. You can easily change veterinarians. You can seek the opinion of specialists without permission from your primary care veterinarian or the insurance company. Second, because veterinarians generally do not bill insurance companies directly, you will have to pay for services and get reimbursed. Third, some pet insurance plans are more inclusive than others; not a single pet health plan is all-inclusive. Some plans have restrictions for coverage of certain breed-related conditions: if your pet happens to be a German shepherd or a Labrador retriever, he or she may not be covered for hip dysplasia. Some pet insurance companies review the patient's medical record and then limit coverage for preexisting conditions. If your pet is receiving allergy injections when you apply for pet insurance, allergy-related expenses may not be covered. Other companies simply don't offer plans with premium coverage to older patients, or they do so at a considerably higher premium. Last, but by no means least, even when a pet insurance policy does cover an illness or injury, all plans have limits. Some plans reimburse a percentage of each visit; other plans have maximum allowances that they will pay out annually for each illness or injury your pet might encounter. Regardless, the set coverage is not always adequate to support your pet until he or she is 100 percent recovered. In fact, depending on the severity of your pet's condition and the type of care you elect to pursue, insurance coverage may be just a minor subsidy in the final cost. Pet insurance can be financially helpful, especially for unanticipated illnesses or injuries; however, having pet insurance does not mean that you will never need to think about the cost of veterinary care.

Some people are financially pragmatic and disciplined enough to create and manage their own pet care fund. I have one client who is retired and lives on a fixed income, but who manages to care for several geriatric cats. He said to me, "My veterinary expenses can be pretty well anticipated; they're stable even when, say, blood work is needed, so I budget for that amount monthly, but I also try and stockpile a bit more so as to accumulate a slush fund for emergencies." This method of essentially providing one's own insurance can prove more financially beneficial and flexible than buying insurance. If you are lucky and your pet is generally healthy for the first ten years of its life, you could save and invest several thousand dollars that would otherwise have been spent on insurance premiums. Of course, if your pet happens to experience illness or injury earlier in life, this pet care fund could be inadequate. You need to budget and make decisions that will work best for your situation.

Having a credit card dedicated solely to pet expenses and care is another type of indemnity. The idea is to maintain a low enough balance and a high enough credit limit to cover any pet emergency that might occur. Of course, interest rates on credit cards can be high, so you will still need to budget for how you will pay down the debt so that the card is recharged for the next unanticipated pet event. CareCredit, Inc. is a finance company that recently began offering loans specifically for veterinary care. Their current offerings include a short-term interest-free loan to qualified applicants, as well as extended payment plans (with interest) for larger veterinary expenses. Again, these are loans that must be repaid in order for lenders to continue assisting others in need.

Veterinarians are generally more sympathetic to clients with limited financial resources when they are up front and honest about what they can afford, demonstrate a sincere effort to help their situation, and are truly committed to their animal companions. I know clients who have postponed or cancelled vacations, taken on extra hours or extra jobs, pawned their belongings, refinanced mortgages and loans, and given up vices in order to support their pets. Most veterinarians are inherently suckers for an animal in need, but they do need to balance their desire to help animals with the financial realities of managing a business. And like most hard-working people, they do not like to be taken advantage of. In the end, our generosity is better spent when we help clients who are truly dedicated to their pets and earnest about helping themselves.

For people who truly do have limited resources and cannot qualify for financing, veterinary care is rarely an all or nothing proposition. It saddens me greatly when people describe situations where they have been given only two options: one really expensive option or euthanasia. For example, if your dog has a broken leg, it might cost $3,000 to repair surgically. If that is an affordable amount of money for you, and surgery is determined to be the best way for getting your pet's leg to heal, then get the operation. However, if that is more money than you can borrow or repay, perhaps the leg will heal with a $300 cast and a lot of rest. Even if the leg has to be amputated for $1,000, that patient will still have one more limb to run with than I do. Cost-saving options usually involve trade-offs, but these may be acceptable to you and your pet, particularly if the only alternative is euthanasia. The point is that a patient does not necessarily need to die because of a lack of money. Be honest and explore cost-saving options with your veterinarian.

Here are more suggestions:

1. Maybe diagnostic tests can be prioritized or performed in stages, and your veterinarian

can get a diagnosis without having to do all of the tests he or she ideally recommends. Obviously this option is more feasible for stable and comfortable patients than for those who are critically ill or in pain. If a patient is ill enough to require hospitaliza-tion, skimping on diagnostics can delay appropriate treatment and prolong recovery.

2. Maybe your pet can be managed as an outpatient, and you can do the nursing care at home and save on hospital fees. Of course, home care may challenge you to learn and perform a few nursing skills on your own pet.

3. Maybe there is an alternative drug that is a little cheaper. Newer drugs are usually more expensive, though not always significantly better than older drugs. Brand-name products are generally more expensive than generics. Shopping around may not be worth the savings if your pet is only going to be on a prescription for a week, but if it is a long-term prescription, the savings may be considerable.

4. Maybe there is another treatment option that will work well enough and cost less given your pet's lifestyle. There are medical, surgical, and radiation therapy options, for

example, for treating feline hyperthyroidism. There are numerous ways to manage and treat dogs with hip dysplasia, ranging from exercise and nutritional supplements to radical reconstructive surgery.

Finally, acknowledging that most of us have financial constraints, I still try not to overplay the cost of veterinary care with my clients. It seems inherently wrong to assign monetary value to a companion's life. Moreover, when we think through some of the other factors surrounding any health care option, such as what we would be asking the patient to tolerate, the potential complications, and the most likely end result, many decisions can be made before cost becomes a necessary or deciding consideration. For example, many people don't want to put their sixteen-year-old dog through radiation therapy once they realize that it requires anesthesia for each of the fifteen treatments. In these cases, the decision is made, as it should be, based on what the patient's body will likely tolerate and how much overall benefit the patient is likely to gain from therapy, rather than on whether or not the clients can afford $3,000 or whether or not the pet is worth $3,000 to them.

When I declared as a teenager that I wanted to be a veterinarian, the first thing I was told was that it was harder to get accepted to veterinary school than to medical school. The second thing I was told was that I would never be rich. If wealth is only measured in dollars, then that was certainly accurate advice. But if bearing witness to sacred moments between humans and animals counts for anything at all, then I am one of the richest human beings on the planet. *Kindred Spirit, Kindred Care* is not about assigning value to a pet's life; it is about making thoughtful decisions on behalf of our animal companions and making financial plans to support that priority.

CHAPTER SEVEN

The Spiritual Nature
of Animals

Even as we gather information about our animal companion's ailment, and as we assess what we can do in practical terms to help our pet, we must also consult our own ethical and spiritual beliefs. The question is not always what *can* we do, but what *should* we do. As medical problems grow more serious, and as our animal companions age, this question can become more urgent and poignant.

Human minds have the capacity to reflect and to ponder: to wonder who we are, why we exist, and what happens after we die. Science has led to a broader understanding about our physical selves — our universe, our solar system, our planet, our chemistry, our biology, and the evolution of our species. For some, only science offers verifiable and provable — "real" — truths about birthing, breathing, and dying. But even though science has not validated the existence of a soul or a spiritual self, many of us find comfort in the idea, perhaps even find it impossible to deny, that there is more to life than organ systems, cellular functions, and biochemical pathways, for ourselves as well as for our animal companions.

Some of my clients grapple with questions pertaining to the spiritual nature of their animal companions and the nature of animal afterlife: Do animals have souls? What happens after they die? Is it wrong to love an animal as much or more than a human? And finally, is euthanasia a humane release from pain and suffering or an immoral taking of life? Sometimes my clients wonder about how the choices they make for their animal companions will affect their own spiritual judgment. I will not tell them what to believe, but I will share my own thoughts about animals, life, and spirituality. Sometimes awareness of other views on the spiritual nature of animals gives perspective to one's own. Understanding the beliefs of others may prompt some to reconsider their own assumptions about animal souls or perhaps develop greater confidence in their actions toward nonhuman life.

For many, religion is the primary source for guidance concerning questions about souls and the afterlife. However, organized religions are overwhelmingly concerned with human spirituality, giving rise to uncertainty about the status of animals. The trend, at least in Western society, appears to lean toward accepting that animals, at least the ones that we come to know more intimately, do have souls, or at least something that makes each of them unique individuals. These animals clearly have sentience, interests, and feelings. These animals can clearly know joy, anxiety, shame, sadness, frustration, rage, and pain, just as humans do. Where there is ambiguity, is it not better too err on the side of spiritual equality? So far as I can tell, humans and animals are biologically more similar than different. As such, why would the afterlife experience that applies to us not apply to them? For humans, religious or spiritual faith does not usually arise from our cognitive minds, but from some other part of our consciousness. As I observe my nonhuman companions as they experience moment-to-moment, uncomplicated, honest emotions and interactions, I wonder whether my cognitive awareness is truly a gift or an unrealized handicap. Perhaps animals are less encumbered and more spiritually attuned than humans.

In some traditions, animal souls and spirits are a certainty that no one even thinks to question. In traditional Hawaiian spirituality, for example, all life and many natural objects and phenomena possess both a physical form and a spiritual form. Spirit or *akua* dwells within human, animal, plant, insect, stone, wind, wave, and the universe at large; the physical form determines the experience of the spiritual form. *Akua* in a bird knows what it feels like to fly; *akua* in a wave is familiar with current, tide, and perpetual motion; *akua* in a shark knows gliding effortlessly through the water; *akua* in the wind knows what it is like to be entwined with all other forms. *Akua* is timeless; death or cessation of a physical form frees the akua to enter a new form or to reenter the spirit universe at large.

The traditional Hawaiian spiritual view upholds a physical world that is much richer than meets the eye, and it perpetuates respect and equality among humans, animals, and nature. Taken a step further, people who perceive death as the release of a spirit from the limitations of a bodily form to a grander existence have fewer fears and misgivings about their own passing or that of an animal companion. While they may still mourn and be saddened by the death of a loved one, they do so with the reassurance that even though the manner of their relationship will change, their spiritual connection will continue.

Accepting that animals have a spiritual nature similar to that of humans can complicate decision-making on behalf of animal companions, especially when considering procedures like organ transplants, cloning, and euthanasia. Unlike human organ donors, animals do not volunteer to donate their organs or their lives to save another member of their species. Some animal organ donors are shelter animals who are then adopted by the recipient's family. In other cases, the donor's life is sacrificed, clearly deemed less significant than that of the recipient. For myself, as much as I love my animal companions, I could not morally sacrifice another animal's life in order to prolong theirs.

Cloning is one of the most fascinating and frightening science projects that humans are engaged in. Imagine being able to produce a genetically identical replica of a beloved pet. These days, at the cutting edge of science and technology, this kind of cloning is a reality. But even the researchers are quick to point out that while cloning replicates genetic make up, it does not preserve the life experiences that made the individual unique. The clone will never be the cloned. It is a reminder that every life is special in and of itself and deserves respect and consideration as such. Our lives, the lives of our animal companions, and the intimate moments we share are precious because we are each unique and neither immortal.

Euthanasia is the deliberate ending of life usually for reasons considered to be merciful. Having witnessed animals in many conditions and states, it is my personal feeling that pain and suffering are worse than dying. However, no one should be coerced into ending the life of an animal companion. Euthanasia of humans is considered first degree murder and is a criminal offense.

Most religions prohibit killing regardless of the circumstances. While veterinarians are licensed to end the life of animal patients, it is an act that is irreversible and should never be decided lightly. Under the correct circumstances, euthanasia can be a selfless gift of mercy and kindness. Euthanasia can also be a violation of a patient's interest in living and a caregiver's commitment to caring for their animal companion.

In our modern society, physical pain can and should be managed. Sometimes a compromised patient may not tolerate the doses of medication necessary to alleviate pain and may die sooner than if the medication had not been administered. In medical ethics, this type of calculated risk is called the Principle of Double Effect: although there is risk of death, the goal is alleviation of pain. Suffering can be more difficult to assess, but should also be a consideration. Supporting our efforts to maintain a good quality of life for our animal companions, chapter 9 addresses ways to recognize and accommodate our pet's special needs and expectations in the face of aging or debilitating ailments. Chapter 10 describes graceful exits with and without euthanasia.

Some of my clients readily accept that their pets have spirits or souls as they do themselves, but this can then progress to a different moral dilemma. If the animals we know as companions have souls, then what about other animals? How much moral responsibility do we have toward protecting other life? Do we allow rodents to help themselves from our kitchens, or fleas to infest our cats and dogs? Where does that spiritually put our carnivorous pets who eat, and may even hunt, other animals? Cats, for example, are obligate carnivores and require the animal-derived amino acid taurine to survive.

Perhaps the indigenous people of the planet offer the most balanced perspective of human-animal interactions. For the most part, indigenous people see themselves as both physically and spiritually part of the circle of life. Yes, animals have spirits and should be respected. However, all animals, human and nonhuman alike, must eat to live. Appreciating and honoring the life that is to be sacrificed for food or other use is more characteristic than guilt or remorse. Taking life unnecessarily is generally taboo; legends abound of humans who have been severely punished for wanton or unnecessary killing.

Alas, being an intelligent, reflective, and creative species in the natural world implies a duty to make spiritually responsible decisions. If human behavior toward animals is consistently governed by respect and kindness, then it seems we will be doing what is best for our own spiritual destinies, as well as the spiritual destinies of the animals with whom our lives intersect.

CHAPTER EIGHT

Making a Decision

By now we have assessed our pet's ailment — and any other conditions or peculiarities that might complicate his or her ability to deal with that ailment or the treatment for that ailment (chapter 4). We also have an understanding of the therapeutic treatments for that ailment, what each option will require of our pet and ourselves, the expected outcome for each option, and the potential complications for each option (chapter 5). We have also examined the financial commitment that the treatment options will entail and pondered our own values and any other factors that might affect our choices (chapters 6 and 7). Last but by no means least, we have an appreciation for our animal companion as a unique individual with certain interests of his or her own that we want to recognize and respect in the process of making the best decisions that we can on his or her behalf (chapters 1 and 2). All of the necessary information that you could possibly need to make a sensible decision on behalf of your pet is now crammed into your brain and onto those pages of notes about your diagnosis and treatment options.

For some of you, my work is done. Some people have an innate capacity to process volumes of new information and confidently make decisions; others will, once they understand their pet's situation and the available treatment options, trust the ultimate recommendation of their veterinarian, particularly if he or she is familiar with them and their pet. However, many people may still be uncertain about what to do for their ailing animal companion, and this chapter presents a systematic way to work through your options and make the best decisions.

Six yes-or-no questions follow. After each are directives for what to do with the option if you've answered "yes" and what to do if you've answered "no." You will either continue to the next question or put that option aside and continue to the next option. After each set of directives, I've inserted text to clarify the purpose of the question.

For each option, start with Question 1. The questions are ordered in a way that filters out the choices that are not going to work for your animal companion before challenging you with more in-depth deliberations. If your option does not "pass" Question 1, then the answers to the rest of the questions don't matter. Options that "pass" all six questions are likely to be good choices for you and your companion animal. It is still a good idea to evaluate all of your options since sometimes implementing more than one treatment may yield an even better end result.

If you are uncertain but leaning toward an option, then go to the next question. If you are uncertain but leaning *away* from the option, then put the option aside and go to the next option. If you have worked through all of the options and not found a suitable one, you may need to modify your priorities or objectives.

Question 1. Does your pet have a concurrent condition that would prohibit or undermine the benefits of this option?

- *If you answer "yes" to Question 1, then put the option aside and go to the next option.*

- *If you answer "no" to Question 1, then go to Question 2.*

Consider a pet with compromised kidneys. Fluid therapy is a principal means of treating and supporting these patients; we might offer or administer twice the volume of fluids that the patient would normally require in order to flush accumulated toxins from his or her system. If the patient also has a heart condition, however, we might have to modify our treatment plan so that we don't stress the compromised heart with the additional fluids. Modifications might involve administering smaller volumes of fluid more frequently or providing additional medications to support the heart. A heart condition would also be associated with considerably higher risk for options like dialysis or kidney transplant. Even an animal's diet needs to be selected more carefully for patients with multiple ailments.

Sometimes when there are lots of concurrent conditions to think about or an ailment is imminently life-threatening, we are challenged to pursue certain options in spite of the risk. We must make a calculated risk, and this usually requires a very trusted veterinarian and close monitoring. I've experienced the calculated risk situation most frequently in patients with the descriptively named condition "trench mouth." Typically, this involves a geriatric patient who is generally doing quite well for having a few compromised organ systems, which are being managed with drugs and supportive care. However, the patient also has halitosis, tartar build-up, and gingivitis but has not demonstrated discomfort or difficulty eating (in fact, has never missed a meal). Under the circumstances, many clients choose to live with their pet's bad breath rather than risk the anesthesia necessary for dental hygiene. When the risk is significant, such a decision is certainly not unreasonable. Occasionally, however, the dental disease develops into a more serious threat to the patient: tooth abscesses can be so painful that the patient refuses to eat or drink, and trench mouth can seed life-threatening infections to kidneys or heart valves, landing patients in the emergency room. In these situations, the patient's life is threatened, and we might not be able to cure the patient without assuming the anesthetic risk to deal with the underlying dental issues. One could argue that performing procedures earlier while the patient is more stable is better than waiting till the patient's life is seriously threatened. Alternatively, one could argue that if we pursue the procedure sooner and things go awry, we will compromise or shorten the patient's life even more.

Question 2. Will your pet be excessively stressed by or intolerant of the treatment and thus undermine the benefits of this option?

- *If you answer "yes" to Question 2, then put the option aside and go to the next option.*

- *If you answer "no" to Question 2, then go to Question 3.*

Remember, no one enjoys being a patient. We can rationalize about the hoped-for benefits of health care and proceed as gently as possible, but patients will still exercise different degrees of resistance to handling and medical procedures. Sometimes the stress of administering a medication might offset or outweigh the intended benefits. For example, you should ask yourself if a treatment is truly being beneficial if you need to search every nook and cranny for your cat companion, drag him out by a limb, chase him around a bit, pounce on him, wrap him up in a blanket, pry his locked jaws open, and hope he will swallow the pill prescribed to keep his blood pressure down.

Even the most accommodating pets are likely to start avoiding you if you are continually approaching them with pills, eye drops, ear wipes, ointments, injections, and/or supplements day after day. Can you blame them? Some treatments contribute significantly to a patient's health and survival, while others might be prophylactic or not as critical. You might need to prioritize which treatments are the most necessary and balance science with compassion and common sense in order to achieve healing and well-being.

Question 3. Will your animal companion appreciate the benefit as much as you will?

- *If you answer "no" to Question 3, then put the option aside and go to the next option.*
- *If you answer "yes" to Question 3, then go to Question 4.*

Question 3 is the second half of the cost-benefit analysis that you are doing on behalf of your pet (the cost analysis having been answered in the previous question). This is the question that prevents us from making selfish decisions. Animals, like humans, appear to have different interests. Some clearly demonstrate tenacity to life, a determination to survive, and a refusal to die without a fight. Others seem more resigned to whatever fate awaits them, and they are resistant to intervention, inconvenience, and bother. If you pursue and are successful with an unpleasant treatment, what will the quality of life be for your pet during it and/or afterward, and will that be acceptable to him or her? For those of us most committed to the health and longevity of our animal companions, this question can be the most difficult to answer honestly. Sometimes when I consider what I would want if I were the patient, the answer is very different from the one that I would choose as a caregiver or care provider. As much as I am committed to the longevity of my animal companions, I know that I need to make decisions based on their interests as well.

Question 4. Are the potential side effects and complications acceptable to you?

- *If you answer "no" to Question 4, then put the option aside and go to the next option.*
- *If you answer "yes" to Question 4, then go to Question 5.*

Question 4 ensures that no matter what happens, we will not be haunted by our decisions. If the worst-case scenario were actually to occur, could you and your animal companion handle it? Would you sincerely believe that "at least we tried" or "we did the best we could," or would you be haunted by regret? If you are prepared to deal with the potential consequences, then your choice is a calculated risk, not a fool's gamble.

Consider one of my canine patients diagnosed with mouth cancer. The type of cancer she had is notoriously aggressive, and without treatment it likely would have become debilitating within three to six months. Unfortunately, the suggested cancer treatment was not so attractive either, involving radical surgery that would remove a section of the dog's upper jaw, cheekbone, and one eye, followed by fifteen treatments of radiation. At the time, not enough patients with the same type of cancer had undergone the extensive therapy to accurately predict how much it might extend her life.

During one of my conversations with her people, I expressed concern that if the treatment didn't work, or if there were significant complications, the patient could end up spending a lot of her remaining time laid up in a hospital rather than enjoying the familiar comforts of home. I would have felt terrible if the treatment itself were to shorten her life or diminish its quality. My clients, on the other hand, perceived that their dog wanted to live. They understood that the treatments were complicated and risky and might not extend their animal companion's life significantly. However, it was important to them to support their dog's interest in living and fighting her cancer, rather than passively succumbing to its sentence, and they were prepared to deal with the adverse consequences if they needed to. In the end, eighteen months, one surgeon, two oncologists, one acupuncturist/herbalist, and one dentist later, she was still pack leader, going for walks, delighting in home-cooked meals, and basking in the sun.

Question 5. Do you find this option ethically acceptable?

- *If you answer "no" to Question 5, then put the option aside and go to the next option.*
- *If you answer "yes" to Question 5, then go to Question 6.*

Advanced medical technology sometimes gives rise to the question, "Just because we can, does it mean we should?" Consider transplants, for example, which involve harvesting an organ. In veterinary medicine, the "donor" is usually a shelter animal or a purpose-bred animal that will either be sacrificed or possibly adopted by the recipient pet's people. It is fairly common for kidney "donors" to be adopted; heart "donors" clearly do not survive. At some level, it is amazing what we can do to prolong the life of a beloved pet, but at what cost to another animal or to our humanity?

Some people find euthanasia morally objectionable. As I discuss in greater depth in chapters 7 and 10, I personally feel that prolonged pain and suffering are worse than dying; however, no one should be coerced into ending life, and there are drugs to control pain and suffering when euthanasia is not an acceptable option.

Question 6. Can you support this option in terms of your time, resources, and capacity for nursing care?

- *If you answer "no" to Question 6, then put the option aside and go to the next option.*

- *If you answer "yes" to Question 6, then the option is likely to be a good choice for you and your animal companion.*

Question 6 asks us to be honest about our values, obligations, and limitations. For example, spinal injury patients sometimes become paralyzed, partially or fully, depending on the location and degree of the injury. Some will require diapers or catheters. With appropriate treatment, therapy, and time, a respectable percentage of paralyzed patients will recover. Others will improve but remain handicapped. Some will remain permanently disabled.

As a doctor evaluating a paralyzed patient, it is often impossible to predict which patients will recover and which ones will not. Like disabled people, many of these animals can have an excellent quality of life with appropriate care and support. It would be great to give all of them a chance, but not every person has the patience, resources, or capacity to support a handicapped pet. Wheelcarts are custom-built and not usually free of charge. It is no small task to lift a large dog into a wheelcart. And once in the cart, a dog needs to be supervised to make sure that the cart doesn't get its wheels caught on obstacles or otherwise tip over, resulting in further injury. Managing incontinent animals of any size means that you will have contact with bodily excretions regularly.

If these patients don't receive proper care, it can become animal negligence or even cruelty to keep them alive. If no one is available to keep their diapers clean and dry, then diaper rash can develop into horrible infections. Without proper bedding and regularly shifting the patient's position, bedsores can develop into festering wounds or gangrenous infections. Without frequent stretching, movement, exercise, and rehabilitative therapy, joints can stiffen and muscles can weaken, further complicating recovery. Some people have the experience or decisiveness to know what they can handle. Others learn what they can handle by taking on the challenges that face them. Sometimes it is only after trying that we realize that we over-committed. Sometimes we surprise ourselves with our creativity, determination, and tenacity. To evaluate this for yourself, consider what you will lose if you take on a treatment option's financial and/or home-care burdens, and then what you will lose if you don't.

Finally, remember that the act of making decisions on behalf of our animal companions is an ongoing process. The best decisions are subject to follow-up. Our pet's condition can certainly change; perhaps his or her tolerance will change; perhaps our resources or capacity to care for our pet will change; and perhaps experience will change our views or values. With any of these changes, our options and choices might change as well. In any situation, we need to make decisions in order to focus our energy and accomplish goals. But we should also occasionally reevaluate our choices in order to ascertain that our decisions continue to be the right ones over time.

CHAPTER NINE

Managing Needs
and Expectations

I n chapter 2, we acknowledged that animal communication is primarily nonverbal. Despite the lack of
words, amazing human-animal bonds can develop when
we let go of our human egocentrism and allow ourselves
to become familiar with nonhumans. When we pay
attention to body language, facial expressions, and behavior, animals can begin to enhance our lives and
broaden our horizons. Animals can teach us how to
appreciate and celebrate life. Nowhere is this lesson more
important and poignant than when we are confronted
with our animal companion's aging and mortality.

For the most part, it is the nature of animals to age gracefully. Animals don't obsess about graying, vision and hearing loss, or even slowing down. They simply carry on. That is not to say that animals are not bothered by change. I would venture to guess that given a choice, most animals would prefer to be svelte and on top of their game. Nonetheless, animals do not wallow in self-pity, anger, resentment, or fear about what they are not. Animals tend to put on their best face, carry on, and maintain a positive spin on their situation. Animals are generally so good at enjoying life that it is often strikingly apparent when they are uncomfortable or unhappy.

My observations of cat and dog patients old enough to get a driver's permit are that their needs change as they journey through life. What do we do when our animals have less drive or stamina to chase the ball, swim, jump on the kitchen counter to investigate what's for dinner, bark at the neighbors, or keep the territory free of squirrels? What can we do to make life as good as possible for our animal companions as their bodies change? How do we deal with blindness, hearing loss, decreased mobility, dietary restrictions, exercise intolerance, incontinence, or confusion? How can we communicate our ongoing care, appreciation, and love? When it becomes our turn to provide joy, hope, promise, and loyalty, how do we rise to the challenge?

Animals in compromised states don't always spell out their wants. Perhaps it is resignation or simply acceptance of their situation. Perhaps they don't have the energy. Perhaps it is because they are unfamiliar with the options. Indeed, humans these days are generally ill-prepared for health crises or aging gracefully themselves, never mind their animal companions. Advancements in science and medicine have led to denial that all life is temporary. Many people have not had to face death or care for a terminally ill patient in their home. As a society lacking that experience, there is a chasm in our understanding of how to deal with the feelings, opinions, needs, and wants of our patients, as well as with our own emotions in these situations.

Once again, my patients and their caretakers have shown me the way. Little deeds can go a long way toward reassuring animal companions that they are safe and loved. What follows are some specific thoughts and advice for you to consider as you care for your special pet:

- In the face of changing bodies and changing needs, animals appreciate the comfort of a familiar and safe environment. For most of us, home is a sanctuary. Home is where we can be ourselves, let our guard down, and relax. Home is where we breathe slower and more regularly, where our heart rates and blood pressures are lowest, where we produce the least amount of adrenaline and the highest amount of endogenous opiates (those substances your body produces that make you feel good), and where a stressed body can channel its finite resources toward healing. When patients need to spend time away from home, bringing their bed, blanket, stuffed animal, or something bearing the smell and feel of home can provide surrogate comfort.

- Vision and hearing loss are not uncommon in geriatric patients. Fortunately, the process tends to begin later in life and progress very slowly, much like it does with humans, many of whom eventually require reading glasses, bifocals, and hearing aids. Some of these aids are becoming available for pets; however, even without them, pets often compensate brilliantly for their age-associated handicaps. Even with diminished vision and hearing, animals can have phenomenal awareness of what is happening around them. In a familiar environment, animals don't need to depend so much on their vision to know where everything is located. Your smell, along with the unique vibration of your footsteps, alerts your pet when you are near, approaching, or leaving. Even though you may not need to make any adjustments to the environment or your behavior, a few subtle alterations can go a long way in maintaining a quality of life for pets with decreased vision and hearing:

1. Leave the furniture arrangement alone.

2. Minimize obstacles your pet might trip over.

3. Brighten the lights.

4. Invest in gates so that your pet does not stumble into danger zones or down a flight of stairs.

5. Deaf animals still understand body language and can learn hand signs.

6. A lot can be communicated through touch: reassurance, encouragement, concern.

7. Even with decreased vision and hearing, pets often enjoy going out for a sniff. Remember that you are your pet's eyes and ears. Please use a leash.

• Smell and taste often remain functional as long as there is breathing. Mouthwatering home-cooked meals can enhance most anyone's day. Nevertheless, please heed dietary restrictions, as they were recommended for a reason; we certainly don't want a good

meal to harm our animal companion. Consult
with your veterinarian if you are uncertain
about how your pet will tolerate any ingre-
dients. Also, if your pet will be consuming
home-cooked meals almost exclusively for
the long term, you should purchase a book
about balancing meals for your pet and/or
consult with a veterinary nutritionist.
The latter can formulate recipes that
accommodate all of your pet's unique
nutritional requirements.

- Remember to offer love and acceptance
  every day. In a crisis, some people busy
  themselves with tasks and chores. These
  tasks are certainly important, but it is
  equally important to reassure the patient
  that he or she is and will be loved, no
  matter what happens. So what if the entire
  house is not spotlessly clean or the laundry
  is a little backed up? So what if the holiday
  cards are late this year? The patient is not
  likely to be concerned with these matters.
  Play a little, sit together, breathe in
  synchrony, look deeply into each other's eyes,
  and know that your souls have touched.
  Sometimes it is hard to confront our
  sadness and be with our ailing companions;
  however, letting them know how we feel
  about them and continuing to give of

ourselves in the face of adversity is the greatest gift of all. Recognize that each day is a gift and make the best of it.

- Patient care can test our patience and endurance, especially when the diagnosis takes us by surprise, when things do not go as planned, and/or when we desperately want our animal companions to get better. Illnesses and injuries can be stressful on the entire family. In order to provide the best care for our pets in their time of need, we also need to take care of ourselves. Sometimes we need to give ourselves a break. Delegating chores or taking an afternoon off is not a sign of weakness; we perform better when we are rested. Sometimes stepping back for even a few hours allows us to refresh, which translates into generating more positive energy in our caregiving.

- Practice creative pain management. Very few animals or people relish pain. It is much easier to enjoy life when your body is not screaming at you. Facilitate your animal companion's innate desire to carry on. In general, less pain medication is necessary when patients are relaxed and otherwise happy. Offering comfort does not always involve administering medicines.

1. Orthopedic beds offer creaky joints and atrophied muscles a cushioned landing pad and place to rest.

2. In the hands of an accomplished practitioner, acupuncture, massage, chiropractic, and reiki can provide drug-free comfort, and/or they can decrease the level of drug intake.

3. Grooming can contribute to a sense of well-being, especially for animals who maintained themselves meticulously in health or youth and are having a difficult time keeping up. Cats retired from scratching posts can suffer toenails that grow into their toe pads, which cause infected and painful sores.

4. Area rugs provide more traction than hardwood or tiled floors.

5. Ramps can be much easier than stairs, especially to go outside several times daily. Astroturf weathers well and provides excellent traction. For cats, consider relocating litter pans to a site that is easier for them to get to.

- Be aware of and care for any increasing confusion or anxiety in your animal companion. Like human minds, animal minds can also deteriorate. Confusion, disorientation, anxiety, and emotional neediness can develop, and these manifest as separation anxiety, excessive vocalization, nervous incontinence, pacing (and falling), trembling, panting, drooling, not eating or drinking, and/or just plain hysteria. As with the other signs of aging, brain deterioration thankfully tends to develop later in life and progress slowly. Nonetheless, it can be emotionally draining to observe our once vital animal companion mentally melting down. Once again, there are pharmacologic and nonpharmacologic methods for managing confusion and anxiety:

1. For some animals, having a regular schedule can be reassuring. Without as much bladder or bowel control, a pet will be less anxious if it knows that someone will be back in time for the next walk or meal. Similar to puppies, older pets may need more frequent walks and reassurances. You might consider recruiting pet sitters, neighbors, friends, and family, depending on the other demands in your life.

2. Create a soothing, stable, and calm environment. Some animals will really

relax given a comfortable bed, calming aromas, soft lighting, and/or soothing background music.

3. Sometimes relieving pets of their responsibilities allows them to relax. For example, formal assignment or not, most dogs consider it their job to guard the house, especially when home alone. Separation anxiety can develop when they are less capable of performing this function. For some individuals, putting them in a crate or a confined space when you are not there relieves them of guard duty and gives them permission to relax.

4. Sometimes going for a long walk or engaging in some activity that wears your pet out a little will prompt him or her to nap while you attend to other things.

5. Herbal pet relaxants can have a soothing effect on some animals. Check with your veterinarian before trying them, since occasional adverse reactions and side effects can occur.

• Use drugs appropriately to minimize suffering. Pain and anxiety management is an art that requires frequent patient assessment and working as a team with your veterinarian. Like people, animals have individual responses and tolerances to drugs. Some patients are acutely sensitive to pain, while others ignore it and go on. Some patients control their anxiety, while others are overwhelmed by it. Some patients prefer to be narcotized, while others prefer to maintain control of their bodies. Some patients experience greater side effects than relief with drugs and the benefits need to be carefully weighed against the risks.

- Maintain a sense of humor about bodily functions and life. All life-forms poop and pee, sometimes with control and sometimes not.

I share one final thought in regard to managing needs and expectations: do not be too confident in predicting outcome. I have witnessed canine, feline, and avian amputees that are so well adapted, it is difficult to pick them out of a group of full-bodied cohorts. I have witnessed animals so adjusted to wheelcarts that they outrun people and other animals. I have witnessed animals walk after months of paralysis and numerous expert opinions that they would never regain function. I have witnessed patients rebound from radical procedures. I have witnessed miraculous cancer remissions. I have witnessed numerous patients thriving beyond any-one's expectations (my humble self included) given their diagnosis. I have also witnessed patients dying when least expected. I have been humbled too often to be cocky about the absoluteness of science and medicine. I just try to support patients and healing. It is the animals who are the true role models for aging gracefully, adapting to change, and carrying on.

CHAPTER TEN

Graceful Exits

M ost people do not want to talk or even think about dying. Conversations about death are depressing, unsettling, and involve too many unknowns. While it is certainly more pleasing to focus on life and living rather than death and dying, part of my role as a veterinarian is to facilitate graceful exits.

Even though animals exhibit a propensity for enjoying life and aging gracefully, death is not always graceful or dignified. While we all hope that our animal companion will live a full life and die peacefully in his or her sleep, we may be challenged to deal with intractable symptoms, pain, and suffering as organ systems fail. At some point, the failure may advance in such a way that no form of medicine or healing will provide adequate support. At this stage, regardless of intervention, the patient's ability to carry on will noticeably decline. Difficult and undeserved as it is, there may be a time toward the end of our animal companion's life when we are forced to make some of the most difficult decisions on its behalf.

The most difficult part of dying is letting go. Especially for the most committed humans and animals, the transition from doggedly prevailing over a disease to accepting the inevitability of death feels akin to giving up and accepting failure. There does come a time, however, when no further life of quality can be coaxed from a dying body. Even when death is inescapable and imminent, some animals will linger on, enduring considerable pain and suffering in the process. Sometimes they are worrying about you. Sometimes they are simply waiting for permission to let go. In these situations, reassuring our beloved companions that it is okay to die can facilitate a more peaceful passing.

How might we accomplish communicating these reassurances of love, acceptance, and permission to our animal companions? Recall that animals have an aptitude for nonverbal communication. Reassure them in the same manner that you have been reassuring them all their lives, and they will get it. Love them in the same manner that you loved them before and through their illness, and they will know it. Do they know what is happening? Does it frighten them? Do they comprehend the complexity of making decisions on their behalf? Do they understand that we are letting them go because we don't want them to suffer anymore? It is unlikely that your animal companion's mind is burdened by such complicated thoughts. Instead he or she will know the most important things: your sincerity, your selflessness, your compassion, and your love.

Even when given permission to let go, some animals insist on clinging to the remnants of a dying body. Do we accept this tenacity to life despite the pain and suffering it entails, or do we relieve the pain and suffering at the expense of life? As in all other decisions made on behalf of our animal companions, the best answers are individually tailored to medical condition, personality, interests, past experiences, and support system. The person most familiar with the affected animal is usually the one most qualified to assess the situation, though that can be an overwhelming responsibility and involve intense emotions. Remember that others are there for support, including your trusted veterinarian. Even in death, animals have a way of bringing people together.

How liberally should pain medication be used in terminally ill patients? Sometimes in order to maintain comfort, patients end up so heavily sedated that they are barely conscious and at increased risk for respiratory or cardiac arrest. Nevertheless, for me, terminally ill patients are entitled to pain relief even if it unintentionally hastens their death. There is no humanity in passively watching a dying patient suffer needlessly. In human medicine, terminal morphine drips or their equivalent are a fairly common practice that maintains patient comfort and allows the final moment of life to be determined naturally. In veterinary medicine, most clients decide that it is neither prudent nor practical to maintain an animal life without quality or hope of recovery. Again, though, such decisions involve very personal choices.

As most people are aware, veterinarians are licensed to euthanize animals. Being able to end life is one of the most sobering aspects of being a veterinarian. If the patient were human, the same act in most of America would be considered first-degree murder. The decision to euthanize a pet at all, or when its life is no longer worth preserving, is a well-weighted responsibility. Moreover, once the act is performed, it is irreversible.

To me, clients opposed to euthanasia should not be coerced into doing so. A coerced or premature decision to euthanize an animal companion may end up haunting the client and arousing suspicion, distrust, and resentment toward the veterinarian. It is very sad to me when new clients explain that they just can't bear to go back to the veterinarian who put their last pet to sleep. Losing a beloved animal companion is difficult enough as it is; clients do not need to additionally suffer uncertainty about their choices or distrust of the veterinarian who was involved with the patient's passing.

When I discuss euthanasia with clients, it is never as a medical treatment option. Euthanasia is the deliberate taking of life. The most common method utilized in companion animals is a barbiturate overdose, usually by injection. Following administration of the drug, the patient's heartbeat and breathing cease within minutes. Under the right circumstances, euthanasia can be an act of mercy and kindness, to preserve dignity and effect a graceful exit from this life. Euthanasia can also be a violation of the patient's interest in living — a forced and unnatural ending about which feelings of anxiety, failure, and guilt can linger long after the patient is gone. What makes the same act good or bad, right or wrong, selfless or selfish? What are the legitimate justifications for taking life from our animal companions?

Fulfilling the following criteria does not mean that the patient should be euthanized. The act of taking life should never be regarded lightly or decided automatically. Rather, these are some of the situations when there are at least clear and compelling justifications for euthanizing a companion animal:

- The animal patient has a terminal and irreversible disease for which there is no cure, and the disease is causing intractable pain and suffering. Sometimes these animals seem ready to die and seeking to do so with dignity. Trusting in your ability to understand your nonhuman companion's nonverbal communications to you can be difficult and even frightening when misreading your animal companion involves such sober consequences. On the other hand, compelling such an animal to continue living can be a selfish indulgence.

- The animal patient has a terminal and irreversible disease for which there is no cure, and the disease poses a potential threat to the health or well-being of others — for example, rabies.

- The animal companion has attacked and harmed others without provocation or reason, and he or she poses an unmanageable threat to public safety.

There are other situations when euthanasia may be a justifiable option to certain people. It would be the responsibility of the attending veterinarian to ascertain that the client understands the gravity of the action and will not look back on it with regret.

Diminished quality of life is a phrase often brought up when considering euthanasia. What constitutes quality of life? When is life of such diminished quality that it is no longer worth preserving? Once again, the answers differ in each case, but at some level, quality of life is what we make it. I know paralyzed animals that do not appear the least bit displeased with their quality of life, nor do they appear to be wanting to die. I have observed blind and deaf animals trucking along next to their seeing-eye human. I know animals who are a bit confused about where they are and what they should be doing, yet they certainly do not appear distraught as they are gently nudged along by their humans. When these animals happen to have moments of clarity, familiar companions are there to greet them and reassure them that all is well and good in the world.

Commitment aside, what if you physically can't lift or carry your large disabled pet? What if you can't drive or don't have a car? What if you can't quit your job in order to be with your animal companion and provide round-the-clock nursing care? What if you really can't finance four- and five-figure veterinary bills? Sometimes what we can realistically provide simply does not match up to our animal companion's needs. It can become cruel and unusual punishment for both you and your animal companion to battle on in the face of impossible logistics. In some cases, our circumstances may exact an earlier exit than we would otherwise choose for our animal companions. Yes, harsh reality. But at least our animal companions have someone who cares enough to consider the viable options and make the best decision on their behalf.

Finally, exits are not always graceful. Sometimes life ends abruptly and unexpectedly. Sudden deaths can be mixed blessings. The one who died did not have to endure prolonged suffering. Unpleasant medical diagnostics and procedures were avoided. No difficult decisions were necessary. On the other hand, we didn't have a chance to prepare ourselves. We never got to say goodbye. Unexpected deaths are a reminder that each moment is a gift. While we ought not develop an obsession with dying, we might live in such a way that whatever happens next, we will be at peace with ourselves.

CHAPTER ELEVEN

Finding Peace

A fter a companion animal passes away comes the period for self-healing. Losing an animal companion, partner, friend, or soul mate can leave you feeling forsaken with deep, unimaginably painful wounds. For most people, time has a way of healing these metaphorical wounds, replacing the voids with scar tissue that allows us to carry on and face the remaining challenges in our destiny. Self-healing does not mean that you stop loving your animal companion. It means that you accept the change to your relationship whereby you remain in your physical body and your animal companion does not. You and your animal companion may still be very connected through memory and in spirit.

Self-recovery progresses more easily when we know that we made the best decisions possible on behalf of our animal companion. But be warned, it is the nature of the human mind to reflect, to question, and to second-guess, even when a person has thoughtfully and thoroughly deliberated every choice beforehand. What if we had done one more treatment? What if we had chosen a different drug? What if we had not done the surgery? What if we had? Either way, there is no way of predicting the future, or knowing with absolute certainty what might have been. We assess the situation. We assess the options. We make the best possible choices we can, given what we know at the time. Perhaps if we were faced with a similar dilemma again, we might make different choices, but the situation could never be exactly the same because our past experiences would change it. The more important detail, no matter what the outcome, is to be involved in the decision-making process, advocating on behalf of your beloved's interests.

Not everyone is fortunate enough to meet and connect with an animal soul mate. The grief that a person experiences when that companion passes away can be overwhelming. I have witnessed animal passings where I am certain that a part of the person died right along with the animal companion. Until one has experienced such an intense connection with an animal, it can be difficult to comprehend the intensity of the grief that accompanies the separation. Dealing with this type of loss is indescribable: it is a fight like no other to accept the way things are. It may be small consolation, but is true nonetheless, that not everyone will be so blessed as to experience such a connection with another being, human or animal. Such an experience is a gift well worth the pain it costs.

It can facilitate self-healing to memorialize our beloved animal companions. Perhaps it is simply cathartic to acknowledge the special bond that you shared. Perhaps it is a rejection of the idea that our beloved's life was all for naught, that she or he was "just a pet." Maybe we are part of a grander project and a greater movement. Maybe humans fortunate enough to connect with animals should share the experience with others, until these bonds are recognized and honored by all. Change occurs in small steps, and if enough people in our society can recognize companion animals as kindred spirits deserving of kindred care, perhaps such consideration will be extended to other animals in farms, zoos, laboratories, and all the earth's ecosystems. In a democratic society, if a majority of the populace demands change, then change can occur.

Is it a betrayal of your beloved animal companion to adopt another pet someday? No. It is important to realize that your deceased animal companion was one of a kind and irreplaceable. The bond between you and that animal companion can never be replicated. Indeed, if you adopt another animal companion hoping to re-create the previous relationship, it will not be fair to you, the memory of your beloved, or your new animal companion. It is better to be grateful for what you had and be willing to accept a new and different relationship. It is possible to love more than one animal companion in a lifetime. It is possible to recover from the passing on of more than one animal companion in a lifetime. Moreover, there is a great need for considerate animal caregivers. One day when all the animals on the planet are cared for, then adopting another pet might be construed as selfish hoarding or unfaithfulness. That Eden, however, is presently more dream than reality.

Kindred Spirit, Kindred Care, is less about giving answers than providing the questions and tools to facilitate customized decision-making on behalf of our animal companions. Accepting the fact that we, and our animal companions, are all unique entities, the choices that work best for each of us will also vary. As such, I encourage readers to think for themselves and derive choices that they can live with, knowing that such choices will not always be the same as my own.

If those of us who respect other animal life allow our differences to divide and immobilize us, who will be the stewards of the planet? If those of us who respect our animal companions as kindred spirits allow the criticism of others to intimidate us, then who will provide animals the kindred care that they deserve? My goal is to help and to empower some of the best humans on the planet: those who truly love and respect their animal companions, who want to be responsive and responsible pet caregivers, and who want to make the best decisions on behalf of their animal companions.

Aloha aku, aloha mai
(breathe as one with the universe).

Acknowledgments

I never imagined that I would be inspired to write a book. There are many books out there, and not all of them are worth the trees that were sacrificed to print them. But fate and a few human contacts have nurtured in me a veterinarian with something to say that will hopefully, in some small way, make the world a better place for animals and the humans who care about them.

I am infinitely grateful to Professor Paul Deane for his mentoring, encouragement, and feedback through all of the early drafts of *Kindred Spirit, Kindred Care.* Even though I have always wanted to do something that would more broadly benefit animals and the humans who care about them, and even as I recognized the potential for a book about decision-making on behalf of animal companions, I questioned whether I could author such a book. I feared criticism from those who do not share my values. As I battled commitment, serendipity engaged me in a series of correspondences with Professor Deane through which I was reminded that discord is part of scholarly discourse. Even as I have to deal with others' contentions, they have to deal with mine. To rile someone passionately enough to respond, whether in agreement or disagreement, is to succeed in engaging a mind. For two years, throughout my writing, Professor Deane provided thoughtful praise and criticism, paragraph by paragraph, chapter by chapter, and draft by draft. I am certain that *Kindred Spirit, Kindred Care* would not be as timely or as good without his support. Even in retirement, he has nurtured my confidence and inspired me to try to make the world a better place for the animals in our midst.

I am also grateful to scholar Mary Ann Violette, especially regarding chapter 7, "The Spiritual Nature of Animals." I initially tried to convince Mary Ann to write this chapter; I thought that as a dedicated pet guardian and graduate of Boston University's School of Theology, she was considerably more qualified than myself in matters of religion and animal souls. Mary Ann politely declined, although she has provided lots of encouragement and materials to ponder. Mary Ann and her husband, Peter, have been my daily sounding boards; both have demonstrated extraordinary patience, composure, and faith as I have worked through good and bad ideas.

Anyone who has attempted to have his or her writing published understands that it is a very involved and competitive affair. That being said, I am immensely grateful to New World Library for supporting *Kindred Spirit, Kindred Care.* In a word, my editor, Jason Gardner, has been a gift. Imagine having someone who understands and appreciates your goal offer his experience and expertise to fast-track your project to a level of excellence and achievement that you were laboriously trying to figure out on your own. Beyond the writing, there is also a team of people involved with cover design, layout, printing, marketing, and distribution that certainly deserves notice. It is all very important work that makes it possible for a book to connect with its audience.

All veterinarians require a place to care for patients, and Dr. Marjorie McMillan provided me an extraordinary nest built with twigs of kindness, caring, wisdom, critical thinking, experience, state-of-the-art technology, and countless tidbits on healing. In veterinary school, we are trained to be objective practitioners of science-based medicine; we distance ourselves from our patients so that our hearts don't interfere with our thinking. The system also nurtures fierce competition, rather than cooperation, among students and professionals. This indoctrination is most unfortunate, as it results in an environment of frustrated veterinarians, preoccupied egos, and worse, patients whose fear and anxiety often go unnoticed. No one enjoys being hospitalized, but when we are working with patients who might not comprehend the motives for our bizarre conduct, we as caretakers should be held to an even higher standard of kindness and compassion. Client trust also needs to be earned, which involves being honest, sincere, caring, involved, and sometimes vulnerable. It takes a tremendous amount of energy to uphold this standard of practice every day. Veterinarians are humans susceptible to laziness, selfishness, resentment, exhaustion, burnout, and every other negative feeling. In spite of the unending demands it entailed, Dr. McMillan created a center for healing animals based on a philosophy that combines state-of-the-art technology with a caring, compassionate, and healing environment. In 1995, I campaigned to work for her, and being part of her practice for nearly a decade played no small part in the veterinarian that I have become.

In 1990, Dr. Roderick Hinman participated in a ceremony of bonding (legally referred to as marriage) with me. It was not my intention to become attached to a human, but with a near-perfect balance of intellect, humility, dignity, kindness, and love, Rod has proven himself a genuine credit to our species. Rod has supported me through most of my adult life, sharing in my frustrations, anxieties, and victories. Not all relationships can sustain the degree of personal, professional, and spiritual growth that I have undergone; change requires that patience, perseverance, and commitment be added to the love of the newly betrothed.

As committed as I am to aging gracefully with this human, it is clear to me that I am the one who is blessed.

Second to last, I am thankful to the clients who have shared their lives with me and who have entrusted their nonhuman soul mates to my care. Finally, I am thankful to my animal patients and companions. It is the animals who have taught me about aging gracefully, recognizing what things are truly important, and being honest. When I am exhausted and overwhelmed by anxious clients, office politics, personal conflicts, or life in general, my animal patients and companions keep me anchored and inspire me to carry on.

Mahalo,
Shannon Nakaya, DVM

Internet Resources

General References

Merck Veterinary Manual: www.merckvetmanual.com

Veterinary Specialties

American Veterinary Dental College: www.avdc.org
American College of Veterinary Dermatologists:
   www.acvd.org
American College of Veterinary Emergency and
   Critical Care: www.acvecc.org

American College of Veterinary Internal Medicine
(includes internal medicine, cardiology, neurology,
and oncology): www.acvim.org
American College of Veterinary Ophthalmologists:
www.acvo.com
American College of Veterinary Radiology and
Radiation Oncology: www.acvr.org
American College of Veterinary Surgeons: www.acvs.org

Alternatives

American Holistic Veterinary Medical Association:
www.ahvma.org
International Veterinary Acupuncture Society:
www.ivas.org
World Small Animal Veterinary Association:
www.wsava.org

Exotic Pets

Association of Avian Veterinarians: www.aav.org
Association of Reptile and Amphibian Veterinarians:
www.arav.org
Herp Vet Connection: www.herpvetconnection.com
House Rabbit Society: www.rabbit.org

Sources and Recommended Reading

Allegretti, Jan, and Katy Sommers, DVM. *The Complete Holistic Dog Book: Home Health Care for Our Canine Companions.* Berkeley: Celestial Arts, 2003.

Cotner, June. *Animal Blessings: Prayers and Poems Celebrating Our Pets.* San Francisco: HarperSanFrancisco, 2000.

Dolan, Kevin. *Ethics, Animals, and Science.* Oxford: Blackwell Science, 1999.

Dudley, Michael Kioni. *Man, Gods, and Nature.* Honolulu: Na Kane O Ka Malo Press, 1990.

Goodall, Jane, and Marc Bekoff. *The Ten Trusts: What We Must Do to Care for the Animals We Love.* San Francisco: HarperSanFrancisco, 2002.

Kaptchuk, Ted J. *The Web That Has No Weaver: Understanding Chinese Medicine.* New York: Contemporary Books, 2000.

Kowalski, Gary. *The Souls of Animals.* 2nd ed. Walpole, NH: Stillpoint Publishing, 1999.

Kübler-Ross, Elisabeth. *On Death and Dying.* New York: Scribner, 1969.

Legood, Giles, ed. *Veterinary Ethics: An Introduction.* London: Continuum, 2000.

Linden, Eugene. *The Parrot's Lament and Other True Tales of Animal Intrigue, Intelligence, and Ingenuity.* New York: Penguin Putnam, 1999.

Masson, Jeffrey Moussaieff, and Susan McCarthy. *When Elephants Weep: The Emotional Lives of Animals.* New York: Delacorte Press, 1995.

McElroy, Susan Chernak. *Animals as Teachers and Healers.* New York: Ballantine Books, 1996.

Munson, Ronald. *Intervention and Reflection: Basic Issues in Medical Ethics.* 6th ed. Belmont, CA: Wadsworth/Thomson Learning, 2000.

Payer, Lynn. *Medicine and Culture.* New York: Henry Holt and Co., 1996.

Rollin, Bernard. *An Introduction to Veterinary Medical Ethics: Theory and Cases.* Ames: Iowa State University Press, 1999.

Schoen, Allen M. *Kindred Spirits: How the Remarkable Bond Between Humans and Animals Can Change the Way We Live.* New York: Broadway Books, 2001.

Tannenbaum, Jerrold. *Veterinary Ethics.* Baltimore: Williams and Wilkins, 1989.

———. *Veterinary Ethics: Animal Welfare, Client Relations, Competition and Collegiality.* 2nd ed. St. Louis: Mosby, 1995.

Index

allergy treatments, 78
alternative healing
  approaches, 59, 64–68,
  140
amputees/amputation, 9,
  72, 81, 116
anesthesia, 19, 48–49, 83,
  97
animal companions
  adoption of, health
    care costs and, 77–78
  as kindred spirits,
    129–31
  as unique individuals,
    7, 14, 94, 129–30
  diet, 19–24
  exercise, 19, 24–25
  exotic, 140
  fairness to, 14–15
  handicapped, care for,
    103–5, 116
  training, 15–19
animal intelligence, 6–8
*Animals as Teachers and
  Healers* (McElroy), 10
animal spirituality
  cloning and, 88, 89
  ethical dilemmas of,
    90–91
  euthanasia and, 86,
    89–90

  organ transplants and,
    88–89
  religion and, 86–87
  souls/spirits and, 87–88
anxiety management, 114–16
aromatherapy, 63
arthritis, 19, 36
aspirin therapy, 36

B

back problems, 19–20
behavior, observing, 26–27
biopsies, 48, 51–52
birds
  body conformation in,
    20–21
  exercising, 25
  obesity and health
    problems in, 19
  special aptitudes of, 8
  time commitment
    required for, 16
  training, 16
blindness, 110–11, 125
blood pressure checks, 48
brain deterioration, 114–16

C

cancer, 70–71
cancer remissions, 33–34,
  71, 116

About the Author

Veterinarian Dr. Shannon Fujimoto Nakaya is a graduate of Wellesley College and Tufts University School of Veterinary Medicine. She has been active in various aspects of veterinary practice for twenty years. She now divides her time between Massachusetts and Hawaii, doing veterinary consulting, relief work, and continuing to develop her skills as a healer. She lives with her husband, two tortoises, five birds, two goats, and one dog. Her website is www.kindredspiritkindredcare.com.